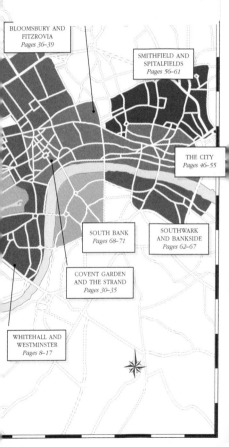

EYEWITNESS TRAVEL
LONDON
POCKET
GUIDE

LONDON, NEW YORK,
MELBOURNE, MUNICH AND DELHI
www.dk.com

PROJECT DIRECTORS Nicholas Bevan, Derek Hall

EDITORS Derek Hall, Sue Juby

DESIGNER Tony Truscott

INDEXER Michael Dent

PICTURE RESEARCHER Mirco De Cet

CARTOGRAPHY John Plumer

Conceived and produced by Redback Publishing,
25 Longhope Drive, Farnham, Surrey, GU10 4SN

Reproduced by Colourscan (Singapore)

Printed and bound in China by Leo Paper Products Ltd.

First published in Great Britain in 2006
by Dorling Kindersley Limited
80 Strand, London WC2R 0RL

Reprinted with revisions 2008

**The information in this
DK Eyewitness Travel Guide is checked regularly.**
Every effort has been made to ensure that this book is as up-to-date as
possible at the time of going to press. Some details, however, such as
telephone numbers, opening hours, prices, gallery hanging
arrangements and travel information, are liable to change. The
publishers cannot accept responsibility for any consequences arising
from the use of this book, nor for any material on third-party websites,
and cannot guarantee that any website address in this book will be a
suitable source of travel information. We value the views and
suggestions of our readers highly. Please write to:
Publisher, DK Eyewitness Travel Guides,
Dorling Kindersley, 80 Strand, London WC2R 0RL.

View of Berkeley Square in Mayfair

CONTENTS

One of the Queen's Life Guards

Central London

Most of the sights in this book lie in Central London. If you are short of time, concentrate on the five areas packed with the most interesting or famous sights: Whitehall and Westminster, The City, Bloomsbury and Fitzrovia, Soho and Trafalgar Square, and Kensington and Chelsea.

National Gallery
Houses one of the world's greatest art collections, including works by da Vinci, van Eyck, Holbein, Vermeer, Velázquez and Monet (see p28).

Tower of London
Built by William I, this riverside fortress became home to the city arsenal, the Crown Jewels, a menagerie and the Royal Mint (see pp52–3).

KEY

Underground station	
Railway station	
River boat pier	

Westminster Abbey
Founded in the 11th century, it has been a place of royal ceremonials ever since. Queen Elizabeth II's coronation was held here, as was the funeral of the Princess of Wales (see pp16–17).

British Museum
The world's oldest museum with over 6 million items spanning 1.8 million years of civilization. The collection includes the Elgin Marbles, the Rosetta Stone and the Amitabha Buddha (see p38).

London's Highlights

Visitors to London are spoiled for choice of things to see and do. Anyone arriving for a short stay, or wanting a flavour of the city, needs to make the most of their time. So here is a time-saving guide to the best London has to offer.

The British Museum visited by over five million visitors a year

Museums and Galleries

British Museum
Contains treasures and artifacts from all over the world *(see p38)*.

National Gallery
This gallery, together with the National Portrait Gallery, make up the core of Britain's art collections *(see p28)*.

Natural History Museum
Life on earth and the earth itself are explained using traditional and interactive exhibits *(see p78)*.

Tate Modern
This exciting gallery covers modern art from 1900 to the present. Highlights include works by Rodin, Rothko and Lucian Freud *(see p65)*.

Imperial War Museum
As well as the weapons of warfare, the museum shows the effects of wars on people's lives *(see p71)*.

Cathedrals and Churches

Westminster Abbey
Since 1066, this royal abbey has been the place where all of Britain's monarchs have been crowned *(see pp16–17)*.

Westminster Cathedral
The Italian-Byzantine Catholic cathedral's red-and-white brick exterior conceals a rich interior of multicoloured marble *(see p14)*.

St Paul's Cathedral
Sir Christopher Wren's Baroque masterpiece, St Paul's has been the setting of many ceremonial events *(see pp48–9)*.

St Martin-in-the-Fields
The only church to have a royal box. The current building was designed by James Gibb in 1726 *(see p28)*.

Southwark Cathedral
This priory church was elevated to a cathedral in 1905. It has many connections with the area's Elizabethan theatres.

The grand west front and towers of St Paul's Cathedral

Shakespeare is commemorated in a memorial and stained-glass window *(see p64)*.

Ceremonies

Horse Guards
During Trooping the Colour, the Queen salutes as a battalion of Foot Guards parades its colours before her *(see p14)*.

Trooping the Colour, one of the most elaborate royal ceremonies

St James's Palace and Buckingham Palace
Members of the Queen's Life Guards stand at the gates of these two palaces *(see pp20–21, 23)*.

Tower of London
In the nightly Ceremony of the Keys, a Yeoman Warder locks the gates. A military escort ensures the keys are not stolen *(see pp52–3)*.

Houses of Parliament
Each autumn the Queen goes to Parliament in the Irish Stage Coach to open the new parliamentary session *(see pp12–13)*.

The Cenotaph
On Remembrance Sunday the Queen pays homage to the nation's war dead, and lays a wreath on the Cenotaph *(see p10–11)*.

Parks

Hyde Park
The Serpentine is one of the highlights of a park which also boasts restaurants, an art gallery and Speaker's Corner *(see p79)*.

Regent's Park
In this fine park surrounded by Regency buildings, you can stroll around the rose garden, visit the open-air theatre, or simply sit and admire the view *(see p86)*.

St James's Park
You can feed the ducks, or watch the pelicans in this royal park. A band plays throughout the summer *(see p24)*.

Hampstead Heath
This breezy open space in North London has excellent views across the city *(see p88)*.

Greenwich Park
Its focal point is the National Maritime Museum, but the park also boasts rolling vistas, broad avenues and other interesting buildings. There are some fine river views *(see p88)*.

Kite flying on one of Hampstead Heath's many pleasant hills

WHITEHALL AND WESTMINSTER

The heart of political and religious power in England for over 1,000 years, Whitehall and Westminster overawe with their pomp and monumental architecture. Situated here are the Houses of Parliament and Westminster Abbey as well as all the major offices of state.

SIGHTS AT A GLANCE

Historic Streets and Buildings
Houses of Parliament pp12–13 ❶
Big Ben ❷
Jewel Tower ❸
Parliament Square ❻
Downing Street ❽
Cabinet War Rooms and Churchill Museum ❾
Banqueting House ❿
Horse Guards Parade ⓫
St James's Park Station ⓭

Churches, Abbeys and Cathedrals
Westminster Abbey pp16–17 ❹
St Margaret's Church ❺
Westminster Cathedral ⓯
St John's, Smith Square

Museums and Galleries
Guards Museum ⓬
Tate Britain ⓰

Monuments
Cenotaph ❼

SEE ALSO

• *Street Life p15*

KEY

🚇 Underground station

🚉 Railway station

◀ *Looking down Whitehall towards Big Ben*

Houses of Parliament ❶

See pp12–13.

Big Ben ❷

Map 5F. Bridge St SW1. Not open to the public.

Big Ben is the name of the 14-tonne bell of the clock in the tower that rises above the Houses of Parliament. Its resonant chimes have kept exact time for the nation more or less continuously since it was first set in motion in 1859.

The four-faced clock, the largest in Britain, home to the bell, Big Ben

Jewel Tower ❸

Map 5F. Abingdon St SW1. Open daily except 24–26 Dec, 1 Jan. Adm charge.

This and Westminster Hall *(see p13)* are the only vestiges of the old Palace of Westminster. The tower was built in 1365 as a stronghold for Edward III's treasure and today houses an exhibition, *Parliament Past and Present*, relating the history of Parliament. Alongside are the remains of the moat and a medieval quay.

Westminster Abbey ❹

See pp16–17.

St Margaret's Church ❺

Map 5F. Parliament Sq SW1. Open daily, but times vary. Free.

A favoured venue for political and society weddings,

A statue of Charles I overlooking St Margaret's doorway

this much-restored early 15th-century church retains some Tudor features, notably a stained-glass window that celebrates the engagement of Catherine of Aragon to Arthur, Henry VIII's eldest brother.

Parliament Square ❻

Map 5F. SW1.

Laid out in the 1840s, the square became Britain's first official roundabout in 1926. It is dominated by statues of statesmen and soldiers, notably Winston Churchill and Abraham Lincoln.

Cenotaph ❼

Map 4F. Whitehall SW1.

This monument was completed in 1920 by Sir Edwin Lutyens to commemorate

The Cenotaph, strewn with poppies

the dead of World War I. Each year on Remembrance Day – the Sunday nearest 11 November – the monarch and other dignitaries place wreaths of red poppies on the Cenotaph. The ceremony honours the victims of World Wars I and II.

No. 10 Downing Street, the official home of the Prime Minister

Downing Street 8

Map 5F. SW1. Not open to the public.

Downing Street was named after a 17th-century entrepreneur, Sir George Downing, who built a street of houses, of which only four survive. King George II gave No. 10 to Sir Robert Walpole in 1732. Since then it has been the official residence and offices of the Prime Minister. In 1989, for security reasons, iron gates were erected at the Whitehall end. The house at No. 11 Downing Street is the official residence of the Chancellor of the Exchequer.

Cabinet War Rooms and Churchill Museum 9

Map 5F. King Charles St SW1. Open daily except 24–26 Dec. Adm charge.

Housing the War Cabinet during World War II, the War Rooms have been maintained exactly as they were, with Churchill's desk, markers and maps for plotting strategy, and communications equipment. The Churchill Museum is a new addition.

Banqueting House 10

Map 4F. Whitehall SW1. Open Mon–Sat except public hols, 24 Dec–1 Jan. Adm charge.

The sole survivor of the fire that destroyed most of the old Whitehall Palace, this was the first building in London to embody the Classical Palladian style that Inigo Jones brought back from Italy. The ceiling paintings by Rubens, an allegory on the exaltation of James I, were commissioned in 1630 by his son, Charles I, who was executed outside Banqueting House in 1649.

Panels from the Rubens ceiling, Banqueting House

Houses of Parliament ❶

Since 1512 the Palace of Westminster has been the seat of the two Houses of Parliament, the Commons and the Lords, and is where the government formulates legislation. The present building is a Gothic revival structure from 1870.

Peers *are members of the House of Lords – many receive their titles for services to their country. This is their lobby.*

The Commons' Chamber *seats the Government on the left, the Opposition on the right, and the Speaker on a chair between them.*

Members' entrance

The Tower *is 106 m (320 ft) high and houses a huge four-faced clock, whose bell is called Big Ben.*

The Mace *is the symbol of royal authority in the House of Commons. It rests on a table between the sides of the House.*

The Royal Gallery *is where the Queen passes through at the State Opening of Parliament.*

The Lords' Chamber *has a throne from which the Queen delivers a speech at the State Opening.*

The Central Lobby *has a ceiling of rich mosaics.*

St Stephen's entrance

Westminster Hall *is the only surviving part of the original Palace of Westminster and dates from 1097; its hammer-beam roof is 14th century.*

VISITORS' CHECKLIST

Map 5F. London SW1.
Tel 020 7219 3000. House of Commons Visitors' Galleries and House of Lords' Visitors' Galleries open daily when House is sitting. Guided tours by appointment. Free.
www.parliament.uk

Horse Guards Parade ⑪

Map 4F. Whitehall SW1. Open daily. Changing the Guard and Dismounting Ceremony daily. Trooping the Colour: June. Free.

These elegant buildings were completed in 1755. On the left are the Old Treasury, and Dover House completed in 1758 and now the Scottish Office. On the opposite side, next to the Admiralty, is the ivy-covered Citadel, a bomb-proof structure built in 1940.

Mounted sentry stationed outside Horse Guards Parade

Guards Museum ⑫

Map 5E. Birdcage Walk SW1. Open daily except Christmas period. Adm charge.

A must for military buffs. Tableaux and dioramas illustrate battles in which the Guards have taken part, from the English Civil War to the present. Weapons, uniforms and models are on display.

St James's Park Station ⑬

Map 5E. Broadway SW1.

Built into Broadway House, this was Charles Holden's 1929 headquarters for London Transport. The station has sculptures by Jacob Epstein and reliefs by Henry Moore and Eric Gill.

Jacob Epstein sculpture located outside St James's Park Station

Westminster Cathedral ⑭

Map 5E. Ashley Place SW1. Open daily. Adm charge for bell tower.

A rare Byzantine building in London, Westminster Cathedral was designed for the Catholic diocese and completed in 1903. Its 87-m (285-ft) high red-brick tower, with horizontal stripes of white stone, contrasts with the Abbey (*see pp16–17*). Eric Gill's reliefs of the 14 Stations of the Cross adorn the nave, the widest in Britain.

St John's, Smith Square ⑮

Map 5F. Smith Sq SW1. Open to the public for concerts.

A masterpiece of English Baroque architecture, Thomas Archer's plump church, with its turrets at each corner, looks as if it is

Premier Ensemble at St John's, Smith Square

trying to burst from the confines of the square. Today it is principally a concert hall. Completed in 1728, it was burned down in 1742, struck by lightning in 1773 and destroyed by a World War II bomb in 1941. There is a reasonably priced basement restaurant open daily for lunch and on concert evenings.

Tate Britain 16

Map 6F. Milbank SW1. Open daily except 24–26 Dec. Adm charge for special exhibitions only.

The world's largest collection of British art from the 16th to 21st centuries is here, from Elizabethan portraiture to cutting edge installations. The Clore Gallery houses the stunning Turner Bequest, left to the nation by the great artist J M W Turner. Highlights include Turner's tribute to David Wilkie *Peace – Burial at Sea*, J A M Whistler's atmospheric night scene *Nocturne in Blue and Gold: Old Battersea Bridge* and Francis Bacon's anguished vision in *Three Studies for Figures at the Base of the Crucifixion*.

Tate Britain, built in 1897 by the sugar magnate, Sir Henry Tate

STREET LIFE

RESTAURANTS

The Cinnamon Club
Map 5F. The Old Westminster Library, Great Smith St SW1. Tel 020 7517 9898.
Expensive
Innovative Indian cuisine served in club-like premises.

Tate Britain Restaurant
Map 6F. 4 Millbank SW1. Tel 020 7887 8825.
Moderate
Open for lunch only.

See p96 for price codes.

PUBS AND CAFÉS

Westminster Arms and Storey's Wine Bar
Map 5F. 9 Storeys Gate SW1.
Hosteries often freqented by politicians.

Footstool
Map 5F. St John's, Smith Square SW1.
Good for a lunchtime snack.

SHOPPING

Parliamentary Bookshop
Map 5F. 1 Parliament SW1.
Parliament-related souvenirs.

Westminster Abbey ❹

The Abbey is world-famous as the resting-place of Britain's monarchs, and has been the setting for all coronations since 1066. Within its walls can be seen some of the most glorious examples of medieval architecture in London.

The West Front Towers *were completed in 1745.*

Flying Buttresses *transfer the great weight of the 31-m (102-ft) high nave.*

The Nave, *viewed here from the West End, is the highest in England.*

The Cloisters *were built mainly in the 13th and 14th centuries.*

The Lady Chapel has a superb vaulted ceiling and choir stalls dating from 1512.

Victorian Stonework adorns the main entrance.

The North Transept's three chapels on the east side contain some of the Abbey's finest monuments.

St Edward's Chapel houses Edward the Confessor's shrine and the tombs of other English monarchs.

The Chapter House has 13th-century tiles.

Museum

VISITORS' CHECKLIST

Map 5F. Broad Sanctuary SW1.
Tel 020 7222 5152.
Cloisters open daily; Abbey open Mon–Sat; Chapter House & Museum open daily. Adm charge. College Garden open Tue–Thu. Evensong daily; times vary. Concerts.
www.westminster-abbey.org

The South Transept contains "Poets' Corner", with memorials to famous literary figures, such as Shakespeare and Dickens.

PICCADILLY AND ST JAMES'S

Piccadilly is the main artery of the West End. The area is famous for being the location of many royal parks, landmarks and buildings, including Buckingham Palace. Mayfair to the north is still the most fashionable address in London, while Piccadilly Circus marks the start of Soho.

SIGHTS AT A GLANCE

Historic Streets and Buildings
Piccadilly Circus ❶
Burlington Arcade ❹
Ritz Hotel ❺
Spencer House ❻
St James's Palace ❼
St James's Square ❽
Royal Opera Arcade ❾
Pall Mall ❿
The Mall ⓭
Clarence House ⓮
*Buckingham Palace
pp20–21* ⓯

Museums and Galleries
Royal Academy of Arts ❸
Institute of Contemporary
Arts ⓫
Queen's Gallery ⓰
Royal Mews ⓱

Churches
St James's Church ❷

Parks and Gardens
St James's Park ⓬

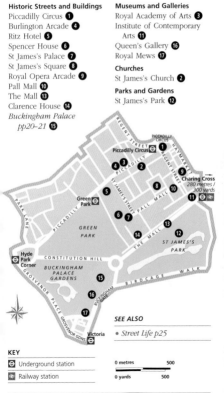

SEE ALSO

• *Street Life p25*

KEY

🔵 Underground station

✠ Railway station

| 0 metres | 500 |
| 0 yards | 500 |

◀ *Piccadilly Arcade with its many fine shops*

Buckingham Palace

Buckingham Palace is both office and London residence of the Queen and her husband, the Duke of Edinburgh. It was built as a town house for the first Duke of Buckingham in 1705. John Nash extended it into a substantial palace, which was first occupied by Queen Victoria in 1837.

The Royal Standard *flies from the palace when the Queen is in residence.*

The Green Drawing Room *is the first of the state rooms entered by guests at royal functions.*

The Music Room *is where state guests are presented and royal christenings take place.*

The State Dining Room *hosts meals which are less formal than state banquets.*

Kitchen and staff quarters

The Queen's Gallery *often displays works from the Queen's Collection.*

The Royal Mews *runs along the west side of the Palace.*

The Extensive Front *was completed by Sir Aston Webb in 1913.*

The Throne Room *is illuminated by seven magnificent chandeliers.*

The Changing of the Guard *takes place in summer, as the palace guard is changed in a colourful and musical ceremony.*

The Palace Balcony, *from where the Royal Family waves to eager crowds.*

Court post office

The Blue Drawing Room *has imitation onyx columns created by John Nash.*

VISITORS' CHECKLIST

Map 5E. SW1. Tel 020 7321 2233. State rooms open Aug–Sep daily. Changing of the Guard: daily Apr–Jul; alternate days Aug–Mar. Tel 0906 866 3344 (Visit London). Adm charge. **www.royalcollection.org.uk**

Alfred Gilbert's statue of Eros

Piccadilly Circus ❶

Map 4E. W1.

For years people have congregated under the figure of Eros – almost a trademark for the capital – erected in 1892. Piccadilly Circus now consists mainly of shopping malls. The circus also boasts London's gaudiest array of neon advertising.

St James's Church ❷

Map 4E. Piccadilly W1. Open daily. Free.

Designed by Wren, this church has been altered over the years and was half

Ornate organ in St James's Church

wrecked by a bomb in 1940, but it maintains its essential features from 1684 – the tall, arched windows, thin spire (a 1966 fibreglass replica of the original) and a dignified interior. The ornate screen behind the altar is one of the finest works by the 17th-century master carver Grinling Gibbons.

Royal Academy of Arts ❸

Map 4E. Piccadilly W1. Open daily except 24–25 Dec. Adm charge.

The courtyard in front of Burlington House, one of the West End's few surviving mansions from the early 18th century, is often crammed with people waiting to see one of the visiting art exhibitions on show at the Royal Academy (founded 1768). The annual summer exhibition comprises around 1,200 new works by both established and unknown artists. There are permanent items in the sculpture promenade outside the galleries, notably a Michelangelo relief of the *Madonna and Child* (1505)

Burlington Arcade ❹

Map 4E. Piccadilly W1.

One of four 19th-century arcades of small shops which sell traditional British luxuries. (The Princes and Piccadilly Arcades are on the south side of Piccadilly, while the Royal Opera Arcade is off Pall Mall.) The arcade is still patrolled by beadles who make sure an atmosphere of refinement is maintained.

Ritz Hotel ⑤

Map 4E. Piccadilly W1.
Open to non-residents.

Swiss hotelier Cesar Ritz,
who inspired the adjective
"ritzy", had this hotel built
and named after him in
1906. The colonnaded
frontal aspect of the
château-style building was
meant to suggest Paris,
where the grandest hotels
were to be found. A popular
place for genteel afternoon
tea, with daily servings in
the chic atmosphere of the
Palm Court.

Spencer House ⑥

Map 4E. St James's Pl SW1. Open
Sun. Garden: open one Sun in
June. Closed Jan & Aug. Adm
charge. No children under 10.

This Palladian palace, built
in 1766 for the first Earl
Spencer, an ancestor of the
late Princess of Wales, has
been completely restored to
its 18th-century splendour.
It contains some wonderful
paintings and contemporary
furniture; a highlight is the
beautifully decorated
Painted Room.

St James's Palace ⑦

Map 4E. Pall Mall SW1. Not open
to the public.

Built by Henry VIII in the
1530s, this is the building
in which Queen Elizabeth
II made her first speech as
queen in 1952. Foreign
ambassadors are still officially accredited to the
Court of St James's. Its
northern gatehouse is one
of London's most evocative
Tudor landmarks. Behind it

St James's Tudor gatehouse

the palace buildings are
occupied by privileged
Crown servants.

St James's Square ⑧

Map 4E. SW1.

One of London's earliest
squares, it was laid out in
the 1670s and lined by
exclusive houses. Many of
the buildings date from the
18th and 19th centuries.
There are some lovely
gardens in the middle of
the square.

William III's statue in St James's Square

Royal Opera Arcade 9

Map 4E. SW1.

London's first shopping arcade was designed by John Nash and completed in 1818, behind the Haymarket Opera House (now called Her Majesty's Theatre). It beat the Burlington Arcade by a year or so.

Royal Opera Arcade

Pall Mall 10

Map 4E. SW1.

For more than 150 years Pall Mall has been at the heart of London's clubland. Here exclusive gentlemen's clubs were formed to provide members with a refuge from their womenfolk. The clubhouses bear testimony to the most fashionable architects of the era.

Institute of Contemporary Arts 11

Map 4E. The Mall SW1. Open daily, but times vary. Charge for non-members.

Established in 1947 to offer British artists some of the facilities available to artists at the Museum of Modern Art in New York. Originally on Dover Street, it has been situated in John Nash's Classical Carlton House Terrace (1833) since 1968. It has a cinema, auditorium, bookshop, art gallery, bar and restaurant. It also offers plays, concerts and lectures.

St James's Park 12

Map 5E. SW1. Open daily. Concerts on summer weekends.

In summer, office workers sunbathe between the flower beds of the capital's most ornamental park. Once a marsh, it was drained by Henry VIII and incorporated into his hunting grounds. Charles II added an aviary on its southern edge (hence the name Birdcage Walk, where the aviary was once situated).

Early summer in St James's Park

The Mall 13

Map 4E. SW1.

This triumphal approach to Buckingham Palace was created by Aston Webb in 1911. It follows the course of the old path at the edge of St James's Park, laid out in the reign of Charles II. The flagpoles on both sides of The Mall fly national flags of foreign heads of state during official visits.

Clarence House 🄮

Map 4E. Stable Yard SW1. Open Aug–mid-Oct. Adm charge.

Designed by John Nash for William IV in 1827, this is Prince Charles's London home. Once a year, the public has access to the opulent ground floor.

Buckingham Palace 🄯

See pp20–21.

Queen's Gallery 🄰

Map 5E. Buckingham Palace Rd SW1. Open daily except 24–25 Dec. Adm charge.

The Queen has one of the world's finest and most valuable art collections, rich in the work of old masters, including Vermeer and Leonardo da Vinci. The gallery has been expanded in the most extensive addition to Buckingham Palace in 150 years. One of the rooms has a permanent display of some of the royal collection's masterpieces.

Aston Webb's Victoria Monument, outside Buckingham Palace

Royal Mews 🄱

Map 5E. Buckingham Palace Rd SW1. Open Mar–Oct. Adm charge.

Open for a few hours each day, the Mews is a must for lovers of horses and royal pomp. The stables and coach houses accommodate the horses and coaches used by the Royal Family on state occasions. The gold state coach, built for George III in 1761, is the star exhibit.

STREET LIFE

RESTAURANTS

The Wolseley
Map 4E. 160 Piccadilly W1.
Tel 020 7499 6996.
Moderate
Refined à la carte and café menus.

ICA Café
Map 4E. The Mall SW1.
Tel 020 7930 8619.
Moderate
Good food at reasonable prices.

See p96 for price codes.

PUBS

Red Lion
Map 4D. Waverton St W1.
Tel 020 7499 1307.
A traditional pub serving bar snacks. Restaurant at rear.

SHOPPING

Gieves and Hawkes
Map 4E. 1 Savile Row W1.
Established in 1785, this is one of the best-known tailors.

Fortnum and Mason
Map 4E. 181 Piccadilly W1.
Upmarket department store.

SOHO AND TRAFALGAR SQUARE

Soho has been renowned for pleasures of the table, the flesh and the intellect since the late 17th century. Soho is also famous as the centre of London's Chinatown, containing scores of restaurants and shops. With a cosmopolitan mix of people, visitors here can enjoy the many sights, bars, restaurants and cafés – popular with everyone from tourists to locals.

SIGHTS AT A GLANCE

Historic Streets and Buildings
Trafalgar Square ❶
Leicester Square ❹
Chinatown ❺
Carnaby Street ❻

Churches
St Martin-in-the-Fields ❷

Galleries
National Gallery ❸

SEE ALSO

• *Street Life p29*

KEY

🅔 Underground station

🚉 Railway station

| 0 metres | 500 |
| 0 yards | 500 |

◀ *St Martin-in-the-Fields on the east side of Trafalgar Square*

Trafalgar Square ❶

Map 4F. WC2.

London's main venue for rallies and outdoor public meetings, now partly pedestrianized, is dominated by the 50-m (165-ft) column commemorating Admiral Lord Nelson, Britain's famous sea lord, who died at the Battle of Trafalgar in 1805.

Nelson's statue

St Martin-in-the-Fields ❷

Map 4F. Trafalgar Sq WC2. Open daily. Free.

Many famous people are buried here, including Charles II's mistress, Nell Gwynne, and the painters William Hogarth and Joshua Reynolds. An unusual feature of the spacious interior is the royal box on the left of the altar.

National Gallery ❸

Map 4F. Trafalgar Square WC2. Open daily except 24–26 Dec, 1 Jan. Free.

In 1824 George IV persuaded a reluctant government to buy 38 major paintings, including works by Raphael and Rembrandt, and these became the start of a national collection. Much of the collection is housed on one floor divided into four wings. Works include *The Hay Wain* (1821) by John Constable, Jan van Eyck's *Arnolfini Portrait* (1434) and *The Ambassadors* (1533) by Hans Holbein.

Leicester Square ❹

Map 4E. WC2.

Residents of this animated heart of the West End included Isaac Newton and William Hogarth. The Victorians established popular music halls here, including the Empire (today the cinema on the site has the same name) and the Alhambra, replaced in 1937 by the Art Deco Odeon. A booth on the square sells cut-price theatre tickets.

Chinatown ❺

Map 4E. Streets around Gerrard St W1.

Much of London's Chinese community moved from the East End at Limehouse into Soho during the 1950s, where they created an

Trafalgar Square and the National Gallery

ever-expanding Chinatown. It contains scores of restaurants, and mysterious aroma-filled shops selling oriental produce. Three Chinese arches straddle Gerrard Street, where at the end of January a colourful street festival celebrates Chinese New Year.

Carnaby Street ⑥

Map 3E. W1.

During the 1960s this street was the centre of "swinging London". After years of neglect, the street is once again gaining a reputation for cutting-edge fashion.

Traditional Chinese New Year celebration, Chinatown

STREET LIFE

RESTAURANTS

Harbour City
Map 4E. 46 Gerrard St W1.
Tel 020 7439 7120.
Moderate
Authentic Cantonese cooking.

Alastair Little
Map 3E. 49 Frith St SW1.
Tel 020 7734 5183.
Expensive
Seasonal and eclectic modern European cooking.

Itsu
Map 3E. 103 Wardour St W1.
Tel 020 7479 4794.
Moderate
Oriental conveyor-belt restaurant.

New World
Map 4E. 1 Gerrard Place W1.
Tel 020 7734 0396.
Moderate
Renowned for its selection of dim sum served from a trolley.

See p96 for price codes.

PUBS AND CAFÉS

The Dog and Duck
Map 3E. 18 Bateman St W1.
Friendly Victorian pub.

The Cork and Bottle
Map 4E. 44–46 Cranbourn St WC2.
1970s basement wine bar with bistro food.

Patisserie Valerie
Map 3E. 44 Old Compton St W1.
Classic Soho café serving delicious cakes and pastries.

SHOPPING

Ann Summers
Map 3E. 79 Wardour St W1.
Rather risqué sex shop.

Merc
Map 3E. 10 Carnaby St W1.
Still sells clothes cut from original 1960s patterns.

Contemporary Ceramics
Map 3E. 7 Marshall St W1.
Inspiring British ceramics.

COVENT GARDEN AND THE STRAND

Open-air cafés, street entertainers, stylish shops and markets make this area a magnet for visitors. At its centre is the Piazza, which sheltered a wholesale market until 1974. Since then, the pretty Victorian buildings here and in the surrounding streets have been converted into one of the city's liveliest districts.

SIGHTS AT A GLANCE

Historic Streets and Buildings
The Piazza and Central Market ①
Neal Street and Neal's Yard ⑥
Savoy Hotel ⑩
Somerset House ⑪
Bush House ⑫
Charing Cross ⑮

Museums and Galleries
London's Transport Museum ③
Photographers' Gallery ⑨

Churches
St Paul's Church ②

Monuments and Statues
Seven Dials ⑧
Cleopatra's Needle ⑬

Famous Theatres
Theatre Royal Drury Lane ④
Royal Opera House ⑤
The London Coliseum ⑯

Parks and Gardens
Victoria Embankment Gardens ⑭

Shopping Arcades
Thomas Neal's ⑦

SEE ALSO

- *Street Life p35*

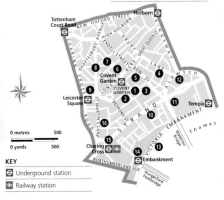

KEY

🔵 Underground station

🚆 Railway station

◀ Enzo Piazotta's statue *The Young Dancer, in Covent Garden*

The Piazza and Central Market ❶

Map 4F. Covent Garden WC2.

Originally an elegant, residential square, based on an Italian piazza, today the buildings on and around the Piazza are mostly Victorian. The roofed market, built for fruit and vegetable wholesalers, now houses an array of small shops and market stalls. Street entertainment is a tradition of the area.

The Piazza and Central Market

St Paul's Church ❷

Map 4F. Bedfor St WC2. Open Mon–Fri, Sun. Free.

Inigo Jones built this church with the altar at the west end, to allow his grand portico to face east into the Piazza. Clerics objected, and so the altar was moved to the east end. Jones went ahead with his original exterior design. Thus the church is entered from the west. In 1795 the interior was destroyed by fire but rebuilt.

London's Transport Museum ❸

Map 4F. The Piazza WC2. Open daily except 24–26 Dec. Adm charge.

The collection shows public transport past and present. The museum also houses some 20th-century commercial art. This museum is excellent for children, with hands-on exhibits, including the opportunity for children to put themselves in the driver's seat of a London bus or an underground train.

Theatre Royal Drury Lane ❹

Map 3F. Catherine St WC2. Open for performances and guided tours. Adm charge.

The first theatre on this site was built in 1663. Nell Gwynne acted there. The present one, by Benjamin Wyatt, was completed in 1812 and has one of the city's largest auditoriums. The theatre now stages blockbuster musicals.

Royal Opera House ❺

Map 3F. Covent Garden WC2. Open for performances and guided tours.

The first theatre on this site was built in 1732, but was destroyed twice by fire. The present opera house was designed in 1858 by E M Barry. John Flaxman's portico frieze, depicting tragedy and comedy, survived from the building of 1809. After extensive renovation, the building reopened for the new millennium, complete with a second auditorium

The Royal Opera House

and new rehearsal rooms for its Royal Opera and Royal Ballet companies. Backstage tours are available, and the Royal Ballet can be seen rehearsing.

Neal Street and Neal's Yard ❻

Map 3F. Covent Garden WC2.

In this attractive street, former warehouses from the 19th century can be identified by the hoisting mechanisms high on their exterior walls. The buildings have been converted into shops, art galleries and restaurants.

The attractive Neal's Yard

Thomas Neal's ❼

Map 3F. Earlham St WC2.

Opened in the early 1990s, this shopping complex has interesting shops ranging from clothes to jewellery and antiques. The Donmar Warehouse theatre is part of the complex.

Seven Dials ❽

Map 3F. Monmouth St WC2.

The pillar at this junction of seven streets incorporates six sundials (the central spike acts as a seventh). Installed in 1989, it is a copy of a 17th-century monument. The original was removed in the 19th century because it had become a meeting place for criminals.

Seven Dials

Photographers' Gallery ❾

Map 4F. Great Newport St WC2. Open daily. Free.

London's leading venue for photographic exhibitions also has regular lectures and theatrical events.

Savoy Hotel ⑩

Map 4F. Strand WC2.

The Savoy pioneered en-suite bathrooms and electric lighting. Attached are the Savoy Theatre, Simpson's English restaurant, and the Savoy Taylor's Guild.

Somerset House ⑪

Map 4F. Strand WC2. Open daily except 24–26 Dec, 1 Jan. Ice rink: open for two months in winter. Adm charge.

Erected in the 1770s as offices, today it houses three art collections – the Courtauld Institute, the Gilbert Collection and the Hermitage Rooms. The courtyard is an attractive piazza with a fountain, classical music concerts and a winter ice rink.

Bush House ⑫

Map 3F. Aldwych WC2. Not open to the public.

This Neo-Classical building, completed in 1935, was designed as manufacturers' showrooms. Since 1940 it has been used as radio studios, and is headquarters of the BBC World Service.

Bush House from Kingsway

Cleopatra's Needle ⑬

Map 4F. Embankment WC2.

Erected in Heliopolis in about 1500 BC, this pink granite monument's inscriptions celebrate the deeds of the pharaohs of ancient Egypt. It was presented to Britain in 1819 and erected in 1878. It has a twin in New York's Central Park. The bronze sphinxes, added in 1882, are not Egyptian. In its base is a Victorian time capsule of artifacts of the day.

Victoria Embankment Gardens

Victoria Embankment Gardens ⑭

Map 4F. WC2. Open daily. Free.

This narrow public park, created when the Embankment was built in 1878, boasts well-maintained flower beds, some statues of British worthies and, in summer, a season of concerts. Its main historical feature is the water gate at its northwest corner, built as a triumphal entry to the Thames for the Duke of Buckingham in 1626.

Charing Cross 15

Map 4F. Strand WC2.

The name derives from the last of the 12 crosses erected by Edward I to mark the funeral route of his wife, Eleanor of Castille, to Westminster Abbey. Today

The new shopping and office block above Charing Cross Station

a 19th-century replica stands in the forecourt of Charing Cross Station. Above the platforms is a shopping centre and office block, completed in 1991.

The London Coliseum 16

Map 4F. St Martin's Lane WC2.

London's largest theatre, this flamboyant building, topped with a large globe, was designed in 1904 by Frank Matcham and equipped with London's first revolving stage. It was the first theatre in Europe to have lifts. Today it is the home of the English National Opera.

STREET LIFE

RESTAURANTS

Rock and Sole Plaice
Map 4F. 47 Endell St WC2.
Tel 020 7836 3785.
Cheap
Best place in central London for traditional fish and chips.

Rules
Map 4F. 35 Maiden Lane WC2.
Tel 020 7836 5314.
Expensive
London's oldest restaurant, famed for pies and oysters.

Belgo Centraal
Map 3F. 50 Earlham St WC2.
Tel 020 7813 2233.
Cheap
Modern Belgian dishes.

The Ivy
Map 3F. 1 West St WC2.
Tel 020 7836 4751.
Expensive
Immaculate brasserie-style food in smart atmosphere.

See p96 for price codes.

PUBS AND CAFÉS

The Lamb and Flag
Map 4F. 33 Rose St WC2.
Cask ales and delicious roasts.

Gordon's Wine Bar
Map 4F. 47 Villiers St WC2.
An ancient dive.

Frank's Café
Map 3F. 52 Neal St WC2.
Family café serving breakfasts, pasta and sandwiches.

SHOPPING

Jubilee Market
Map 4F. Covent Garden Piazza WC2.
Antiques, crafts and clothes.

Penhaligon's
Map 4F. 41 Wellington St WC2.
Traditional English scents for men and women.

Theatre Shop
Map 4F. St Martin's Lane.
CDs, books and sheet music from musicals.

BLOOMSBURY AND FITZROVIA

At the beginning of the 20th century, Bloomsbury and Fitzrovia were the haunts of famous writers and artists and became synonymous with literature, art and learning. The area still boasts the University of London, the British Museum and many fine Georgian squares, but is now also noted for its restaurants and shops.

SIGHTS AT A GLANCE

Historic Streets and Buildings
Russell Square **2**
British Library **4**
St Pancras International
  Station **5**
Fitzroy Square **7**

Museums
British Museum **1**
Charles Dickens Museum **3**
Pollock's Toy Museum **8**

Churches
St Pancras Parish Church **6**

SEE ALSO

• *Street Life p39*

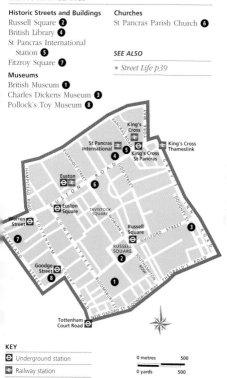

KEY

🚇 Underground station

🚉 Railway station

| 0 metres | 500 |
| 0 yards | 500 |

◄ *A grand Georgian house in Bedford Square*

The imposing entrance to the British Museum

British Museum ❶

Map 3E. Gt Russell St WC1. Open daily. Free.

Established in 1753 to house the collections of Sir Hans Sloane, among the British Museum's exhibits is the 7th-century Sutton Hoo Treasure, the controversial Elgin Marbles and many Egyptian mummies.

Russell Square ❷

Map 3E. Russell Sq WC1.

Russell Square is a lively place, with a fountain, café and roaring traffic. The east side boasts perhaps the best Victorian grand hotel to survive in the capital: Charles Doll's Russell Hotel, from 1900. Poet TS Eliot worked in the square until 1965, in what were the offices of publishers Faber and Faber.

Charles Dickens Museum ❸

Map 2F. Doughty St WC1. Open daily, but times vary. Adm charge.

Novelist Charles Dickens lived in this 19th-century terraced house from 1837 to 1839. His works *Oliver Twist* and *Nicholas Nickleby* were written here, and *Pickwick Papers* was finished here. This is the only one of Dickens's London homes to survive. The museum shows his life and times.

British Library ❹

Map 2F. Euston Rd NW1. Open daily except Good Fri, 24–26 Dec, 1 Jan. Free.

London's most important building from the late 20th century houses the national collection of books, manuscripts and maps, as well as the British Library Sound Archive. It was opened in 1997. A copy of nearly every printed book in Britain is held here – more than 16 million different volumes.

St Pancras International Station ❺

Map 2F. Euston Rd NW1. Open daily.

The extravagant red-brick Gothic frontage of this spectacular rail terminus is technically not part of the station. It was Sir George Gilbert Scott's sumptuous Midland Grand Hotel, which opened in 1874.

The massive former hotel above St Pancras International Station

St Pancras Parish Church ❻

Map 2E. Euston Rd NW1. Open Mon–Fri, Sun. Times vary.

This is a Greek revival church of 1822 by William Inwood and his son Henry, both enthusiasts for

Athenian architecture. The design is based on the Erectheum on the Acropolis in Athens; even the wooden pulpit stands on miniature Ionic columns of its own.

No. 29 Fitzroy Square

Fitzroy Square **7**

Map 2E. Warren St W1.

Designed by Robert Adam in 1794, the square's south and east sides survive in original form, in dignified Portland stone. Blue plaques record the homes of many artists, writers and statesmen: George Bernard Shaw and Virginia Woolf were both occupants of No. 29.

Pollock's Toy Museum **8**

Map 3E. Scala St W1. Open Mon–Sat. Adm charge.

Benjamin Pollock was a renowned maker of toy theatres in the late 19th and early 20th centuries – the novelist Robert Louis Stevenson was a customer. The museum opened in 1956. Exhibits include stages and puppets from Pollock's theatres and a reconstruction of his workshop.

Pearly king and queen dolls from Pollock's Toy Museum

STREET LIFE	
RESTAURANTS	**PUBS**
Pied à Terre	**Fitzroy Tavern**
Map 3E. 34 Charlotte St W1.	Map 3E. 16 Charlotte St W1.
Tel 020 7636 1178.	*The pub that gave its name to*
Expensive	*the area of Fitzrovia. Attracts*
Brilliant modern French	*a lively after-work crowd.*
cuisine and a huge wine list.	
	SHOPPING
Goodfellas	**Jarndyce**
Map 3F. 50 Lamb's Conduit St	Map 3F. 46 Gt Russell St W1.
WC1. Tel 020 7505 7088.	*Antiquarian bookshop.*
Cheap	
Nearest thing to New York-	**Heals**
style deli in London.	Map 3E. 196 Tottenham Court
	Rd W1.
See p96 for price codes.	*Leading furniture store.*

HOLBORN AND THE INNS OF COURT

This area is traditionally home to the legal and journalistic professions. The law remains, but most national newspapers left Fleet Street in the 1980s. Holborn is no longer a main shopping district, but the jewellery and diamond dealers are still here, as are the London Silver Vaults.

SIGHTS AT A GLANCE

Historic Streets, Buildings and Sights
Lincoln's Inn 2
Fleet Street 5
Dr Johnson's House 8
Holborn Viaduct 9
Hatton Garden 12
Staple Inn 13
Gray's Inn 14

Museums
Sir John Soane's Museum 1

Churches
St Bride's 6
St Andrew, Holborn 10
St Etheldreda's Chapel 11

Monuments
Temple Bar Memorial 4

Parks and Gardens
Lincoln's Inn Fields 3

Pubs
Ye Olde Cheshire Cheese 7

Shops
London Silver Vaults 15

SEE ALSO

• *Street Life p45*

KEY

🚇 Underground station

🚆 Railway station

◀ *The Royal Courts of Justice on the Strand*

Sir John Soane's Museum

Sir John Soane's Museum ❶

Map 3F. Lincoln's Inn Fields WC2. Open Tue–Sat except 24–26 Dec, 1 Jan, Easter, public hols. Free. Groups book ahead.

This house was left to the nation in 1837 by leading 19th-century architect Sir John Soane, with a stipulation that nothing should be changed. True to his wishes, the collections are much as he left them – an eclectic gathering of beautiful, peculiar and often instructional objects. The building abounds with architectural surprises and illusions. Among the works are Soane's designs for the Bank of England. Here also is William Hogarth's *Rake's Progress* series.

Lincoln's Inn ❷

Map 3G. Chancery Lane WC2. Open Mon–Fri.

Some of the buildings in Lincoln's Inn, the best-preserved of London's Inns of Court, are late 15th century.

The coat of arms above the arch of the Chancery Lane gatehouse is Henry VIII's, and the heavy oak door is of the same vintage. Ben Jonson is believed to have laid some of the bricks of Lincoln's Inn in the reign of Elizabeth I. The chapel is 17th-century Gothic. Famous alumni include William Penn, founder of the US state of Pennsylvania.

Lincoln's Inn Fields ❸

Map 3F. Holborn WC2. Open daily.

This was a public execution site during the reign of the Tudors and the Stuarts, and many religious martyrs and suspected traitors to the Crown perished here. Today, lawyers come here to read their briefs in the fresh air. In recent years it has also become an evening soup kitchen for London's homeless.

Lincoln's Inn Fields

Temple Bar Memorial ❹

Map 3G. Fleet St EC4.

The monument outside the Law Courts dates from 1880 and marks the entrance to

The dragon, symbol of the City, at the City entrance at Temple Bar

the City of London. On state occasions it is a tradition for the monarch to ask permission of the Lord Mayor to enter. Temple Bar, a huge archway designed by Wren, originally stood here. It is depicted in one of the four reliefs that surround the base of the monument.

Fleet Street ➎

Map 3G. EC4.

England's first printing press was set up here in the 15th century by William Caxton's assistant, and for centuries thereafter Fleet Street was a centre of London's publishing industry. Playwrights Shakespeare and Ben Jonson were patrons of the old Mitre tavern, now No. 37 Fleet Street. Today the newspapers, the agencies Reuters and the Press Association have all left their Fleet Street offices. El Vino wine bar, at the western end opposite Fetter Lane, was a traditional haunt of journalists and lawyers.

St Bride's ➏

Map 3G. Fleet St EC4. Open daily except public hols. Free.

St Bride's is one of Wren's best-loved churches. It has long been the traditional venue for memorial services for departed journalists. Wall plaques commemorate Fleet Street journalists and printers. The octagonal layered spire has been the model for tiered wedding cakes since it was added in 1703. Bombed in 1940, the interior was faithfully restored after World War II. The crypt has remnants of earlier churches on the site, and a section of Roman pavement.

St Bride's, church of the Press

Ye Olde Cheshire Cheese ➐

Map 3G. Fleet St EC4. Open daily.

Parts of this public house date back to 1667, when the Cheshire Cheese was rebuilt after the Great Fire. The diarist Samuel Pepys often drank here in the 17th century, but it was Dr Samuel Johnson's association with "the Cheese" that made it a place of pilgrimage for such 19th-century literati as Mark Twain and Charles Dickens.

Dr Johnson's House ⑧

Map 3G. Gough Sq EC4. Open Mon–Sat. Closed public hols. Adm charge.

Dr Samuel Johnson was an 18th-century scholar famous for his witty and often contentious remarks. Johnson lived here from 1748 to 1759, and he compiled the first definitive English dictionary (1755) in the attic. The house, built before 1700, is furnished with 18th-century pieces and a small collection of exhibits relating to Johnson's life and times.

Civic symbol on Holborn Viaduct

Holborn Viaduct ⑨

Map 3G. EC1.

This Victorian ironwork was erected in the 1860s as part of a much-needed traffic scheme. It is best seen from Farringdon Street, which is linked to the bridge by a staircase. Climb up and see the statues of City heroes and bronze images of commerce, agriculture, science and fine arts.

St Andrew, Holborn ⑩

Map 3G. Holborn Circus EC4. Open Mon–Fri. Free.

The spacious medieval church here survived the Great Fire of 1666.

In 1686 Christopher Wren redesigned it, and the lower part of the tower is virtually all that remains of the earlier church. It was gutted during World War II but faithfully restored as the church of the London trade guilds.

St Etheldreda's Chapel ⑪

Map 3G. Ely Place EC1. Open daily. Free.

This rare 13th-century survivor, the chapel and crypt of Ely House, is where the Bishops of Ely lived until the Reformation.

Hatton Garden ⑫

Map 3G. EC1.

On land that was the garden of Hatton House, this is London's diamond and jewellery district. Gems of all prices are traded from scores of shops with sparkling window displays and even from the pavements.

Staple Inn ⑬

Map 3G. Holborn WC1. Courtyard open Mon–Fri. Free.

This building was once the wool staple, where wool was weighed and taxed. The frontage is the only example of Elizabethan half-timbering left in central London. The shops at street level have a 19th-century feel, and there are 18th-century buildings in the courtyard.

Figure on the façade of St Andrew church

Staple Inn, a survivor from 1586

Gray's Inn ⑭

Map 3G. Gray's Inn Rd WC1. Grounds open Mon–Fri. Buildings by prior arrangement. Free.

This ancient legal centre and law school dates back to the 14th century. Like many buildings in this area, it was badly damaged by World War II bombs, but much of it has been rebuilt. At least one of Shakespeare's plays (*A Comedy of Errors*) was first performed in Gray's Inn hall in 1594. The hall's

16th-century interior screen still survives. The young Charles Dickens worked as a clerk here in 1827–8.

London Silver Vaults ⑮

Map 3G. Chancery Lane WC2. Open Mon–Sat.

London silver has been famous for centuries. These vaults originate from the Chancery Lane Safe Deposit Company, established in 1885. After descending a staircase you pass through formidable steel security doors and reach a nest of underground shops sparkling with antique and modern silverware.

Coffee pot (1716): Silver Vaults

STREET LIFE	
RESTAURANTS	**PUBS AND BARS**
Fryers Delight **Map 3F.** 19 Theobalds Road WC1. Tel 020 7405 4114. Cheap *Traditional fish and chips in an original 1950s setting.*	**El Vino** **Map 3G.** 47 Fleet St EC4. *Popular haunt of journalists and lawyers.*
Pearl **Map 3F.** 225 High Holborn WC1. Tel 020 7829 7000. Expensive *As sumptuous as it sounds.*	**The Punch Tavern** **Map 3G.** 99 Fleet St EC4. *Elegantly decorated. Serves real ales. Frequented by locals.*
See p96 for price codes.	**Ye Old Mitre** **Map 3G.** 1 Ely Court, Ely Place EC1. *Original Georgian era pub serving real ale.*

THE CITY

London's financial district is built on the site of the original Roman settlement. Its full title is the City of London, but it is usually just called the City. It hums with activity in business hours, but few people have lived here since the 19th century, when it was a major residential centre.

SIGHTS AT A GLANCE

Historic Streets and Buildings

Mansion House **1**
Royal Exchange **2**
Old Bailey **5**
Apothecaries' Hall **6**
Tower of London pp52–3 **12**
Tower Bridge **13**
Lloyd's of London **16**

Galleries

Guildhall Art Gallery **17**

Historic Markets

Old Billingsgate **9**
Leadenhall Market **15**

Monuments

Monument **8**

Churches and Cathedrals

St Mary-le-Bow **3**
St Paul's Cathedral pp48–9 **4**
St Magnus the Martyr **7**
St Mary-at-Hill **10**
All Hallows by the Tower **11**

Docks

St Katharine's Dock **14**

SEE ALSO

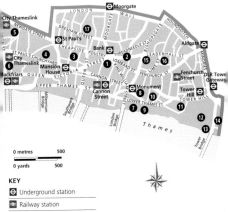

KEY

🚇 Underground station

🚆 Railway station

◁ St Paul's Cathedral

St Paul's Cathedral ❹

Sir Christopher Wren's Baroque masterpiece
dominates the city skyline and has been the setting
for many great ceremonial events. Completed in
1708, it was England's first purpose-built
Protestant cathedral. It has the largest swinging
bell in Europe, which strikes every day at 1pm.

The Towers at the
West Front were added
by Wren in 1707.

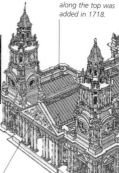

The Balustrade
along the top was
added in 1718.

**The Pediment
Carvings**, dating from
1706, show the
Conversion of St Paul.

The Mosaics on the
choir ceiling were
completed in the
1890s.

The West Porch
is the main entrance
to St Paul's.

**The Geometrical
Staircase** is a spiral
of 92 stone steps
up to the library.

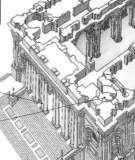

The Dome *is 110 m (360 ft) high – the second biggest in the world after St Peter's in Rome.*

The Whispering Gallery *has unusual acoustics, causing whispers to echo around the dome.*

The High Altar *was based on Wren's original drawings. The canopy over the altar was replaced after World War II.*

North and South Transepts

Entrance to Whispering Gallery

South Porch

Ornate Stone Statuary *can be found situated outside the South Transept.*

VISITORS' CHECKLIST

Map 3H. Ludgate Hill EC4. Tel 020 7236 4128. Cathedral, galleries, crypt and ambulatory open Mon–Sat. Closed for sightseeing Sun. Concerts. Adm charge.
www.stpauls.co.uk

Mansion House ❶

Map 3H. Walbrook EC4. Open to group tours only, by appt. Free.

Completed in 1753, this is the official residence of the Lord Mayor. The Palladian front, with its six Corinthian columns, is a familiar City landmark. Formerly located here were 11 holding cells, a reminder of the building's other function as a magistrate's court. Early 20th-century suffragette Emmeline Pankhurst was held here.

Royal Exchange ❷

Map 3H. EC3. Not open to the public.

Merchant and courtier Sir Thomas Gresham founded the Royal Exchange in 1565 as a place to trade, and Queen Elizabeth I gave it its Royal title. Dating from 1844, this is the third building on the site since Gresham's. Britain's first public lavatories were built in the forecourt in 1855.

The façade of William Tite's Royal Exchange of 1844

St Mary-le-Bow ❸

Map 3H. (Bow Church) Cheapside EC2. Open Mon–Fri, but times vary. Free.

The church gets its name from the bow arches in the Norman crypt. When Wren rebuilt the church (1670–80) after the Great Fire, he continued this pattern through the arches on the steeple. The church was bombed in 1941 but later restored. By tradition, only those born within the sound of the church's bells are Cockneys.

St Paul's Cathedral ❹

See pp48–9.

Old Bailey's rooftop symbol

Old Bailey ❺

Map 3G. EC4. Open Mon–Fri except Christmas, New Year, Easter, public hols. Free.

The new Central Criminal Courts opened here in 1907 on the site of the notorious and malodorous Newgate prison (on special days in the legal calendar judges carry posies to court as a reminder of those times).

Apothecaries' Hall, rebuilt in 1670

Apothecaries' Hall ❻

Map 3G. Blackfriars Lane EC4. Courtyard open Mon–Fri except public hols. Free.

London's livery companies, or guilds, have protected and regulated specific trades since medieval times. The Apothecaries' Society was founded in 1617 for those who prepared, prescribed or sold drugs.

St Magnus the Martyr ❼

Map 4J. Lower Thames St EC3. Open Tue–Fri, Sun, but times vary. Free.

There has been a church here for over 1,000 years. Its patron saint was St Magnus, Earl of the Orkney Islands. Highlights include the carved musical instruments that decorate the organ case.

Monument ❽

Map 4H. Monument St EC3. Open daily except 24–26 Dec, 1 Jan. Adm charge.

The column, designed by Wren to commemorate the Great Fire of London which devastated the original walled city in September 1666, is the tallest isolated stone column in the world. It is 62 m (205 ft) high and

is said to be 62 m west of where the fire started in Pudding Lane. The 311 steps lead to a platform with spectacular views.

Old Billingsgate ❾

Map 4J. Lower Thames St EC3. Not open to the public.

London's main fish market was based here for 900 years. In the 19th and early 20th centuries 400 tonnes of fish were sold here every day, much of it delivered by boat. In 1982 the market moved from this building (1877) to the Isle of Dogs.

Fish weathervane at Old Billingsgate

St Mary-at-Hill ❿

Map 4J. Lovat Lane EC3. Open Mon–Fri, but times vary. Free.

The interior and east end of St Mary-at-Hill were Wren's first church designs (1670–76). The design of the Greek cross was a prototype for his St Paul's proposals. The original delicate plasterwork and 17th-century fittings were lost in a fire in 1988.

Tower of London ⑫

For much of its 900-year history the Tower was an object of fear. Those who had committed treason or threatened the throne were held within its dank walls and often executed. The Tower of London houses the Crown Jewels.

Beauchamp Tower held many high-ranking prisoners.

The Jewel House is where the Crown Jewels are kept.

Tower Green was where aristocratic prisoners were executed, away from the ghoulish crowds on Tower Hill.

The Queen's House is the official residence of the Tower's governor.

A small colony of ravens live at the Tower. Legend states that if they leave, the kingdom will fall. In fact, the birds have clipped wings and cannot fly.

The White Tower, *when it was finished c.1097, was London's tallest building – 30 m (90 ft) high.*

Chapel of St John

The Bloody Tower *is associated with the two princes who disappeared here in 1483.*

Thirty-five Yeoman Warders, *or "Beefeaters", guard the Tower.*

Wakefield Tower

Medieval Palace

Traitors' Gate *was where prisoners entered the Tower by boat.*

VISITORS' CHECKLIST

Map 4J. Tower Hill EC3.
Tel 0870 756 6060; 0870 756 7070 for advance booking.
Open daily (times vary) except 24–26 Dec & 1 Jan. Ceremony of the Keys 9.30pm daily (book ahead).
www.hrp.org.uk

All Hallows by the Tower

Map 4J. Byward St EC3. Open daily except 26 Dec–2 Jan. Adm charge.

The arch in the southwest corner, which has Roman tiles, dates from Saxon times, as do some crosses in the crypt. Samuel Pepys watched the Great Fire from the tower. There is also a brass rubbing centre, a small museum and a bookstall.

Tower of London ⑫

See pp52–3.

Tower Bridge ⑬

Map 4J. SE1. Open daily except 24–25 Dec. Adm charge.

Completed in 1894, this flamboyant project was soon a symbol of London. Its pinnacled towers and linking catwalk support the mechanism for raising the roadway when big ships pass through. The bridge houses The Tower Bridge Exhibition, with interactive displays, river views and a close-up look at the original steam lifting engine.

Neo-Gothic Tower Bridge

The yacht haven of the restored St Katharine's Dock

St Katharine's Dock ⑭

Map 4J. E1. Free.

The dock was designed by Thomas Telford and opened in 1828. By the mid-20th century the docks had declined since they could not handle the large containers carried by ships. St Katharine's closed in 1968. It has since been redeveloped with commercial, residential and entertainment facilities, including a hotel and yacht haven. Old warehouse buildings have shops and restaurants on their ground floors and offices above.

Leadenhall Market ⑮

Map 3J. Whittington Ave EC3. Open Mon–Fri.

Essentially a food market, selling traditional game, poultry, fish and meat, Leadenhall also has a number of shops offering fare ranging from chocolates to wine. At its busiest during breakfast and lunch hours.

Lloyd's of London ⑯

Map 3J. Lime St EC3. Not open to the public.

Lloyd's was founded in the late 17th century and takes

Richard Rogers' Lloyd's building illuminated at night

present building, by Richard Rogers, dates from 1986. Its stainless steel piping and high-tech ducts echo the Pompidou Centre in Paris, which he also co-designed.

Guildhall Art Gallery ⑰

Map 3H. Guildhall Yard EC2. Open daily except 25–26 Dec, 1 Jan. Times vary. Adm charge.

This was built in 1885 to house the art collection of the Corporation of London, but was destroyed in World War II. The present gallery houses the studio collection of 20th-century artist Sir Matthew Smith, and works from the 16th century to the present day, including John Singleton Copley's *Defeat of the Floating Batteries of Gibraltar*. In 1988 the foundations of a Roman amphitheatre, built in AD 70, were discovered beneath the gallery. Access is included with gallery admission.

its name from the coffee house where underwriters and shipowners used to meet to arrange marine insurance contracts. The

STREET LIFE

RESTAURANTS

Sweetings
Map 4H. 39 Queen Victoria St EC4. Tel 020 7248 3062.
Expensive
A lunchtime haven for fish lovers.

Grande Café and Bar
Map 3H. The Royal Exchange EC3. Tel 020 7618 2480.
Moderate
Simple Mediterranean dishes.

Imperial City
Map 3H. The Royal Exchange EC3. Tel 020 7929 6888.
Moderate
Great Chinese cuisine.

PUBS AND CAFÉS

Jamaica Wine House
Map 3H. St Michael's Alley EC3.
Lovely pub dating from 1682 serving bar food as well as wines and beers.

Balls Brothers
Map 3J. 11 Blomfield St EC2.
Old city wine bar serving traditional food.

The Place Below
Map 3H. Cheapside EC2.
Cheap
Lunchtime vegetarian canteen.

See p96 for price codes.

SMITHFIELD AND SPITALFIELDS

This area is one of the most historic in London, containing vestiges of the Roman wall and one of the capital's oldest churches, St Bartholomew-the-Great. This area is also famous for its clothing stalls; Petticoat Lane, a Sunday morning street market that spreads as far east as Brick Lane, is today lined with Bengali food shops and restaurants. Nearby is the Barbican, a late 20th-century residential and arts complex.

SIGHTS AT A GLANCE

Historic Streets and Buildings
Charterhouse ❸
Cloth Fair ❹
Barbican ❻
Broadgate Centre ❽
Petticoat Lane ❾
Fournier Street ⓬
Dennis Severs House ⓭

Churches
St Bartholomew-the-Great ❺
St Giles, Cripplegate ❼
Christ Church, Spitalfields ⓫

Museums and Galleries
Museum of London ❷
Whitechapel Art Gallery ❿

Markets
Smithfield Market ❶
Old Spitalfields Market ⓮

SEE ALSO

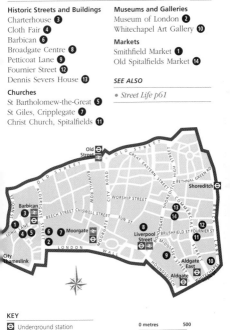

KEY

Ⓔ Underground station

🚉 Railway station

| 0 metres | 500 |
| 0 yards | 500 |

◀ *Columbia Road flower and plant market*

Smithfield Market, officially known as London Central Meat Market

Smithfield Market ❶

Map 3G. Charterhouse St EC1. Open Mon–Fri.

The market was originally sited in Smithfield, outside the city walls, but it moved to its present location in the 1850s and was named the London Central Meat Market. But the former name stuck. The old buildings are by Victorian architect Horace Jones, but there are 20th-century additions.

Museum of London ❷

Map 3H. London Wall EC2. Open daily except 24–26 Dec, 1 Jan. Free.

This museum provides a lively account of London life from prehistoric times to the present day. Exhibits include a working model of the Great Fire of 1666.

Charterhouse ❸

Map 3G. Charterhouse Sq EC1. Open for guided tours only. Free.

The Tudor gateway on the north of the square leads to the site of a monastery which was dissolved by Henry VIII. In 1611 the buildings were converted into a hospital and a school – Charterhouse – whose pupils included John Wesley. In 1872 the school relocated to Surrey. Part of the site was taken over by St Bartholomew's Hospital medical school. Some of the old buildings have survived.

Cloth Fair ❹

Map 3H. EC1.

This pretty street is named after the Bartholomew Fair, the main cloth fair held annually at Smithfield until 1855. Nos. 41 and 42 are fine 17th-century houses and have distinctive two-storeyed bay windows. The former poet laureate John Betjeman lived in No. 43 for most of his life.

17th-century houses: Cloth Fair

St Bartholomew-the-Great ❺

Map 3H. West Smithfield EC1. Open Mon–Sat, times vary. Services Sunday. Free.

The 13th-century arch used to be the door to an earlier church until the nave of that earlier building was pulled down. Today the arch leads

St Bartholomew's gateway

from West Smithfield to the burial ground. The present building retains the crossing and chancel of the original, with its round arches and other fine Norman detailing.

Barbican ⑥

Map 3H. Silk St EC2. Open daily.

This large residential, commercial and arts complex was begun in 1962. Residential tower blocks surround the Barbican Centre, the arts complex, which also includes a lake and fountains. The old city wall turned a corner here and substantial remains are still clearly visible. The

centre has theatres and a concert hall, cinemas, galleries, a library and a conservatory. The Guildhall School of Music and Drama is also in the Barbican.

St Giles, Cripplegate ⑦

Map 3H. Fore St EC2. Open Mon–Fri. Services Sun Easter–Sep.

Completed in 1550, this church survived the Great Fire in 1666, but only the tower survived the ravages of World War II. St Giles was refurbished in the 1950s to serve as the parish church of the Barbican. Oliver Cromwell married Elizabeth Bourchier here in 1620 and the poet John Milton was buried here in 1674. Remains of London's Roman and medieval walls can be seen to the south.

Broadgate Centre ⑧

Map 3J. Exchange Sq EC2.

This is a recent (1985–91) shop and office development. Each of the squares has a distinctive character: Broadgate Arena emulates New York's Rockefeller Center. Among the many sculptures in the complex are George Segal's *Rush Hour Group*, and Barry Flanagan's *Leaping Hare on Crescent and Bell*.

St Giles, Cripplegate

Petticoat Lane ❾

Map 3J. Middlesex St E1.
Open 9am–2pm Sun.

In prudish Victorian times, this street's name was changed to Middlesex Street. However, the old name – derived from years as a centre of the clothing trade – has stuck, and is now applied to the market held every Sunday morning. A great variety of goods is sold, with a bias still towards clothing. The atmosphere is noisy and cheerful, with Cockney stall-holders using their wit to attract custom. There are also scores of snack bars, many selling traditional Jewish food.

Entrance to Whitechapel Gallery

London. In the 1950s and 1960s the likes of Jackson Pollock, Robert Rauschenberg, Anthony Caro and John Hoyland showed work here. In 1970 David Hockney's first exhibition was held here. The gallery has a well-stocked arts bookshop and a café.

Christ Church, Spitalfields ⓫

Map 3J. Commercial St E1. Open Tue, Sun during services. Free.

The finest of Nicholas Hawksmoor's six London churches, completed in 1729, Christ Church still

Petticoat Lane market

Whitechapel Art Gallery ❿

Map 3J. Whitechapel High St E1. Open daily except 25–26 Dec, 1 Jan. Occasional adm charge.

A striking Art Nouveau façade by C Harrison Townsend fronts this light, airy gallery. Founded in 1901, its aim is to bring art to the people of East

Christ Church, Spitalfields

dominates the surrounding streets. The church's impression of size and strength is reinforced inside by the high ceiling, the sturdy wooden canopy over the west door and the gallery. It has recently been fully restored to its former glory.

The grand bedroom of Dennis Severs House

Fournier Street ⑫

Map 3J. E1.

The 18th-century houses on the north side of this street have attics with broad windows designed to give maximum light to the silk-weaving French Huguenot community who lived here. The textile trade lives on, in this and nearby streets – still dependent on immigrant labour.

Dennis Severs House ⑬

Map 3J. Folgate St E1. Opening times vary. Adm charge.

At No. 18 Folgate Street designer and performer Dennis Severs recreated an interior that takes you on a journey from the 17th to the 19th centuries. The rooms are arranged as though the occupants had simply left for a moment.

Old Spitalfields Market ⑭

Map 3J. Commercial St E1. Open daily.

One of the oldest markets in London, Spitalfields started as a produce market in 1682. Today, good quality food can still be purchased here.

STREET LIFE

RESTAURANTS	PUBS
Club Gascon **Map 3G.** 57 West Smithfield EC1. Tel 020 7796 0600. **Expensive** *Top-notch French cuisine.*	**Fox and Anchor** **Map 2J.** 115 Charterhouse St EC1. *A splendid late-Victorian pub.*
	SHOPPING
Carnevale **Map 2H.** 135 Whitecross St EC1. Tel 020 7250 3452. **Moderate** *Excellent vegetarian restaurant. Offers daytime take-away menu.*	**Columbia Road Market** **Map 2J.** Columbia Rd E2. *Plants, flowers, antiques and food. Open Sunday mornings.*
See p96 for price codes.	**Old Spitalfields Market** **Map 3J.** Commercial St E1. *Good food. Clothing, crafts and bric-a-brac on Sundays.*

SOUTHWARK AND BANKSIDE

Shakespeare's company was based at the Globe Theatre, which has been recreated near its original site. The south bank of the river has undergone extensive renovation, and Southwark is once again one of London's most exciting boroughs. Southwark's attractions range from the Design Museum and the Tate Modern, next to the blade-like Millennium Bridge, to historic pubs and Southwark Cathedral.

SIGHTS AT A GLANCE

Historic Streets and Areas
Hop Exchange **2**
The Old Operating
  Theatre **5**
Cardinal's Wharf **7**
Bermondsey **12**

Museums and Galleries
Shakespeare's Globe **6**
Bankside Gallery **8**
Tate Modern **9**
Vinopolis **10**
Clink Prison Museum **11**
London Dungeon **13**
Design Museum **14**

Cathedrals
Southwark Cathedral **1**

Pubs
George Inn **4**

Markets
Borough Market **3**

Historic Ships
HMS Belfast **15**

SEE ALSO

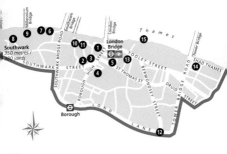

KEY

Underground station

Railway station

| 0 metres | 500 |
| 0 yards | 500 |

◀ The Millennium Bridge located opposite Tate Modern

Southwark Cathedral ❶

Map 4H. Montague Close SE1.
Open daily. Free.

This church become a cathedral in 1905, but some parts are 12th century. A restoration programme has included new buildings with a shop and a café. The exterior has a herb garden and a Millennium Courtyard leading to the riverside.

Shakespeare Window in Southwark Cathedral

Hop Exchange ❷

Map 4H. Southwark St SE1.
Not open to the public.

With easy access to Kent's hops, Southwark was important for brewing beer and trading hops. In 1866 this building was the centre of that trade. Now offices, it retains its original pediment with hop-harvesting scenes.

Borough Market ❸

Map 4H. Southwark St SE1.
Open Thu, Fri, Sat, but times vary.

Borough Market was until recently a wholesale fruit and vegetable market, with origins in medieval times, and moved to its current

The George Inn, now owned by the National Trust

position beneath the railway tracks in 1756. A popular fine food market has now been introduced, selling gourmet foods as well as quality fruit and vegetables.

George Inn ❹

Map 4H. Borough High St SE1.
Open daily.

This 17th-century building is the only traditional galleried coaching inn left in London. It was rebuilt after the Southwark fire of 1676 in a style that dates back to the Middle Ages. Patrons may be entertained by actors and morris dancers.

The Old Operating Theatre ❺

Map 4H. St Thomas St SE1.
Open daily except 15 Dec–5 Jan.
Adm charge.

St. Thomas' Hospital stood here from its foundation in the 12th century until it was moved in 1862. This operating theatre survived. Dating

19th-century surgical tools

The replica Globe Theatre

back to 1822, it is the UK's oldest, and has been fitted out as it would have been in the early 19th century.

Shakespeare's Globe **6**

Map 4H. New Globe Walk SE1. Open daily. Performances mid-May–Sep. Adm charge.

Shakespeare's Globe is a reconstruction of the Elizabethan theatre where many of his plays were performed. The circular structure leaves some of the audience exposed to the weather. Beneath the theatre, and open all year, is Shakespeare's Globe Exhibition, which brings his work and times to life.

Cardinal's Wharf **7**

Map 4H. SE1.

Some 17th-century houses still survive here in the shadow of Tate Modern. A plaque commemorates Christopher Wren's stay here while St Paul's Cathedral was being built. It is thought that the wharf was named after Cardinal Wolsey.

Bankside Gallery **8**

Map 4G. Hopton St SE1. Open daily except 25 Dec–1 Jan. Free.

This modern gallery is the headquarters of the Royal Watercolour Society and the Royal Society of Painter-Printmakers. There are changing displays of water colours and artists' prints. Many pieces are for sale.

Tate Modern **9**

Map 4H. Bankside SE1. Open daily except 24–26 Dec, but times vary. Adm charge for exhibitions.

Tate Modern occupies the converted Bankside power station. Until 2000, the Tate collection was shown at Tate St Ives, Tate Liverpool and the Tate Gallery (now Tate Britain). When Tate Modern joined this family of galleries, space was created for a collection of contemporary art including sculpture, paintings and modern installations. Among important works are Lucian Freud's *Standing by the Rags* (1988–89) and Auguste Rodin's *The Kiss* (1901–4).

Vinopolis

Map 4H. Bank End SE1. Open pm except Wed. Adm charge.

Vinopolis offers interactive and educational exhibits about wine. Within Victorian railway arches, Vinopolis explores the history of the grape and illuminates the process of wine-making. "Tasting stations" provide a chance to savour the subject matter, and choice vintages can be bought after the tour.

Clink Prison Museum ⑪

Map 4H. Clink St SE1. Open daily except 25 Dec. Adm charge.

Now a macabre museum, the prison once located here opened in the 12th century. During the 15th century, it became known as the "Clink", and finally closed in 1780. The museum illustrates the prison's history. Tales of the inmates are told, and hands-on displays of torture instruments leave little to the imagination.

Bermondsey ⑫

Map 5J. SE1. Market open Fri. Fashion and Textile Museum open daily. Adm charge.

Bermondsey's winding streets hold traces of its past in the form of medieval, 18th-century and Victorian buildings. Today it is famous for its antiques market. The Fashion and Textile Museum in Bermondsey Street opened in 2003, and displays British and international fashion, including the collection of designer Zandra Rhodes, from the 1950s to the present day.

Bermondsey antiques market

London Dungeon ⑬

Map 4J. Tooley St SE1. Open daily except 25 Dec. Times vary. Adm charge.

An expanded version of the Chamber of Horrors at Madame Tussaud's, this museum is a great hit with children. It illustrates bloodthirsty events in British history, and activities include live actors and special effects. It is played strictly for terror, and screams abound during enactments of executions and exhibits such as the Great Plague, the Torture Chamber and Jack the Ripper.

Design Museum ⑭

Map 4J. Butler's Wharf, Shad Thames SE1. Open daily except 25–26 Dec. Adm charge.

Founded in 1989, this was the first museum devoted solely to modern and contemporary design. Frequently changing exhibitions explore landmarks in

The ship-like Design Museum

modern design history and the most exciting innovations in contemporary design, set against the context of social, cultural, economic and technological changes. Embracing every area of design, each spring the museum hosts Designer of the Year – a national design prize, with an exhibition at which the public can vote for the winner.

HMS Belfast

Map 4J. Tooley St SE1. Open daily except 24–26 Dec. Adm charge.

HMS *Belfast* played a vital role in World War II. Parts of the ship have been recreated to show what it was like in 1943, when it took part in sinking the German battle cruiser *Scharnhorst*. There are also exhibits about the history of the Royal Navy.

The naval cruiser HMS Belfast has been a museum since 1971

STREET LIFE

RESTAURANTS

Tate Modern
Map 4H. Bankside SE1.
Tel 020 7401 5020.
Moderate
Eclectic menu. Magnificent Thames views to St Pauls.

Fish!
Map 4H. Cathedral St SE1.
Tel 020 7234 3333.
Moderate
Innovative fish dishes in a modern, stylish setting.

Cantina Vinopolis
Map 4H. 1 Bank End SE1.
Tel 020 7940 8333.
Moderate
Excellent Mediterranean food.

See p96 for price codes.

PUBS AND CAFÉS

The Anchor
Map 4H. 34 Park St SE1.
Famous old riverside pub.

Globe Café at Shakespeare's Globe
Map 4H. New Globe Walk SE1.
Located within restored Shakespearean theatre.

SHOPPING

Borough Market
Map 4H. 8 Southwark St SE1.
Good food from all over the country.

Hay's Galleria
Map 4J. Hay's Lane SE1.
Fashion, interiors, bars and open market overlooking the Thames.

SOUTH BANK

As well as the Royal National Theatre and the Old Vic, concert halls and galleries, the South Bank has the National Film Theatre and the IMAX. The South Bank was a focal point for the new millennium, with the raising of the world's highest observation wheel, the London Eye.

SIGHTS AT A GLANCE

Historic Streets and Buildings
Lambeth Palace **6**

Museums and Galleries
Hayward Gallery **2**
Imperial War Museum **7**

Attractions
County Hall **4**
British Airways
London Eye **5**

Theatres and Concert Halls
Royal National Theatre **1**
Royal Festival Hall **3**

SEE ALSO

- *Street Life p71*

KEY

⊖ Underground station	
🚆 Railway station	

0 metres	500
0 yards	500

◀ Thameside promenade on the South Bank

Royal National Theatre

Royal National Theatre ❶

Map 4G. South Bank SE1.
Open Mon–Sat except
24–25 Dec, Good Fri.

Within this innovative building you can see a musical, a classic or a new play in one of its three theatres: the Olivier, the Cottesloe and the Lyttleton. Check for free shows and exhibitions in the foyer. There is also a tour of all three theatres, dressing rooms and workshops.

Hayward Gallery ❷

Map 4F. South Bank SE1. Open daily except 24–26 Dec, 1 Jan, between exhibitions. Adm charge.

This is one of London's main venues for large art exhibitions. Its slabby grey concrete exterior is thought by many as an icon of 1960s "Brutalist" architecture. The new foyer shows a selection of cartoons and artists' videos. Exhibitions cover classical and contemporary art. British contemporary artists are well represented.

Royal Festival Hall ❸

Map 4F. South Bank SE1. Open daily except 25 Dec.

The only structure in the 1951 Festival of Britain designed for permanence, Sir Robert Matthew and Sir Leslie Martin's concert hall was the first major public building in London after World War II. The Royal Festival Hall reopened in 2007 after major refurbishment.

County Hall ❹

Map 5F. Westminster Bridge Rd SE1. Open daily. Adm charge.

Once the home of London's government, the building now houses the London Aquarium, the Saatchi Gallery, a Salvador Dalí exhibition and a computer games hall, plus restaurants, hotels and a health club.

View from the BA London Eye

British Airways London Eye ❺

Map 5F. Jubilee Gardens SE1. Open daily except 25 Dec, Jan. Times vary. Adm charge.

The London Eye is a 135-m (443-ft) high observation wheel. Erected in 2000, it immediately became one of the city's most recognizable landmarks. The 32 capsules take a 30-minute round trip. On a clear day, the Eye affords a unique 40-km (25-mile) view across the capital in all directions and to countryside beyond.

Lambeth Palace ⑥

Map 5F. SE1. Not open to the public.

This has been the London base for the Archbishop of Canterbury, the Church of England's senior cleric, for 800 years. The chapel and its undercroft contain 13th-century elements, but a

Lambeth Palace's gatehouse

large part of the building is more recent. The Tudor gatehouse dates from 1485.

The machinery of war through the ages at the Imperial War Museum

Imperial War Museum ⑦

Map 5G. Lambeth Rd SE1. Open daily except 24–26 Dec. Free.

Despite two colossal guns at the main entrance, this is not just a display of the engines of warfare. Massive tanks, artillery, bombs and aircraft are on show, yet some of the most fascinating exhibits describe how war affects people's lives. The Holocaust exhibition is a permanent display. The museum is housed in part of what was the Bethlehem Royal Hospital for the Insane ("Bedlam").

STREET LIFE

RESTAURANTS

Gourmet Pizza Company
Map 4G. Gabriel's Wharf SE1. Tel 020 7928 3188.
Cheap
Range of pizzas by the river.

Oxo Tower Restaurant Bar and Brasserie
Map 4G. Oxo Tower Wharf SE1. Tel 020 7803 3888.
Moderate
Delicious modern dishes.

See p96 for price codes.

BARS

Fire Station
Map 5G. 150 Waterloo Rd SE1.
Cavernous, popular bar.

SHOPPING

South Bank Centre
Map 4G. South Bank SE1.
Royal Festival Hall and Royal National Theatre shops.

Oxo Tower Wharf
Map 4G. Bargehouse St SE1.
Paintings, ceramics, jewellery, fashion and interiors.

CHELSEA

Chelsea became fashionable in Tudor times, and reached its peak between the 1960s and the 1980s when showy young shoppers paraded along the King's Road. Once the haunt of artists, including Turner, Whistler and Rossetti, who were attracted by the river views from Cheyne Walk, Chelsea is too expensive for most artists now, but the artistic connection is maintained by many galleries and antique shops.

SIGHTS AT A GLANCE

Historic Streets and Buildings
King's Road ❶
Carlyle's House ❷
Cheyne Walk ❹
Royal Hospital ❻
Sloane Square ❼

Churches
Chelsea Old Church ❸

Gardens
Chelsea Physic Garden ❺

SEE ALSO

● *Street Life p75*

KEY

⊖ Underground station	
⊟ Railway station	

0 metres 500
0 yards 500

◀ *Picturesque Chelsea residences in a cul-de-sac off the King's Road*

The Pheasantry, King's Rd

King's Road ❶

Map 6C. SW3 and SW10.

Chelsea's main artery, home of the mini-skirt revolution and punk, still retains its feel for fashion. But today the King's Road also has restaurants such as the Pheasantry, once a hip artist colony, and good antique shops: Chenil Galleries, Antiquarius and Chelsea Antiques Market.

Carlyle's House ❷

Map 7C. Cheyne Row SW3.
Open Wed–Sun, public hols, from Apr–Oct. Adm charge.

The historian Thomas Carlyle moved into this 18th-century house in 1834, and wrote many of his best-known books here, notably *The French Revolution* and *Frederick the Great*. The novelists Charles Dickens and William Thackeray, poet Alfred Lord Tennyson and naturalist Charles Darwin were all regular visitors. The house has been restored and looks as it did during Carlyle's lifetime.

Chelsea Old Church ❸

Map 7C. Cheyne Walk SW3.
Open Tue–Fri, Sun. Free.

Rebuilt after World War II, the glory of this building is its Tudor monuments. One to Sir Thomas More, who built a chapel here in 1528, contains an inscription he wrote asking to be buried next to his wife. Outside the church is a statue of him, gazing across the river.

Cheyne Walk ❹

Map 7C. SW3.

Many of the 18th-century houses of this former riverside promenade remain, bristling with blue plaques celebrating those who have lived in them, including artist J M W Turner who lived at No. 119, writer George Eliot at No. 4, and writers such as Henry James, T S Eliot and Ian Fleming who lived in Carlyle Mansions.

Thomas More on Cheyne Walk

Chelsea Physic Garden in spring

Chelsea Physic Garden ❺

Map 7C. Swan Walk SW3. Open Apr–Oct. Times vary. Adm charge.

Established by the Society of Apothecaries in 1673 to study plants for medicinal use, many new varieties are nurtured in its glasshouses.

Royal Hospital ❻

Map 6D. Royal Hospital Rd SW3. Open daily, except public hols and special functions. Free.

This complex was commissioned by Charles II from Wren in 1682 as a retirement home for soldiers, who are known as Chelsea Pensioners. The hospital is still home to about 330 retired soldiers, whose scarlet coats and tricorne hats date from the 17th century.

Sloane Square ❼

Map 6D. SW1.

This small square has a paved centre with a flower stall and fountain depicting Venus. It was named after physician and collector Sir Hans Sloane who bought the manor of Chelsea in 1712. The Royal Court Theatre is on the west side.

Sloane Square fountain

STREET LIFE

RESTAURANTS

Cactus Blue
Map 6B. 86 Fulham Rd SW3. Tel 020 7823 7858.
Moderate
Southwest American menu.

Sophie's Steakhouse and Bar
Map 6B. 311–313 Fulham Rd SW1. Tel 020 7352 0088.
Moderate
Delicious steaks, fish, burgers, sandwiches and salads.

Bluebird
Map 6C. 350 King's Rd SW3. Tel 020 7559 1000.
Moderate
Great game and shellfish.

PUBS

Chelsea Potter
Map 6C. Kings Rd SW3.
Well-kept, fashionable pub.

King's Head & Eight Bells
Map 7C. 50 Cheyne Walk SW3.
Historic 16th-century pub.

SHOPPING

Conran Shop
Map 6C. Michelin House, 81 Fulham Rd SW3.
Stylish interior goods.

Chelsea Antiques Market
Map 6C. 253 Kings Road SW3.
Busy place packed with stalls.

See p96 for price codes.

SOUTH KENSINGTON AND KNIGHTSBRIDGE

South Kensington and Knightsbridge are among London's most desirable, and expensive, areas. The prestigious shops of Knightsbridge serve their wealthy residents. With Hyde Park to the north, and museums that celebrated Victorian learning at its heart, visitors will find a unique combination of the serene and the grandiose.

SIGHTS AT A GLANCE

Historic Streets and Buildings
Royal College of Music ④
Kensington Palace ⑥

Churches
Brompton Oratory ③

Museums and Galleries
Natural History Museum ①
Victoria and Albert
    Museum ②

Parks and Gardens
Hyde Park ⑦

Monuments
Marble Arch ⑧

Concert Halls
Royal Albert Hall ⑤

SEE ALSO

• Street Life p79

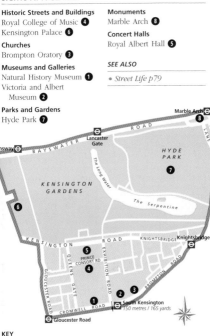

KEY

⊖	Underground station
⊟	Railway station

0 metres   500
0 yards   500

◀ *The Albert Memorial, opposite the Royal Albert Hall*

Natural History Museum ❶

Map 5B. Cromwell Rd SW7. Open daily except 25–26 Dec. Free.

Through a combination of interactive techniques and traditional displays, the Natural History Museum vividly explains life on Earth and even the Earth itself.

Carving at Natural History Museum

Victoria and Albert Museum ❷

Map 5C. Cromwell Rd SW7. Open daily except 24–26 Dec. Free.

The Victoria and Albert Museum contains one of the world's widest collections of art and design, from early Christian devotional objects to cutting-edge furniture. Exhibits include the Great Bed of Ware (*c.*1590) and Tippoo's Tiger (1795).

Brompton Oratory ❸

Map 5C. Brompton Rd SW7. Open daily. Free.

Opened in 1884, this is a rich monument to the English Catholic revival of the late 19th century. All the most eye-catching treasures inside predate the church – many were transported here from Italian churches.

Royal College of Music ❹

Map 5B. Prince Consort Rd SW7. Open Tue–Thu in term-time or by appointment. Adm charge.

Founded in 1882 by George Grove, who also compiled the famous *Dictionary of Music*, pupils have included English composers Ralph Vaughan Williams and Benjamin Britten. In the refurbished Museum of Musical Instruments are instruments from earliest times. Some of the exhibits were played by such greats as Handel and Haydn.

Royal Albert Hall ❺

Map 5B. Kensington Gore SW7. Open for performances. Free.

Completed in 1871, this huge concert hall was modelled on Roman amphitheatres. It is often used for classical concerts, most famously the "Proms", but it also hosts comedy shows, rock concerts, circuses and conferences.

Statue of Prince Albert (1858) outside the Royal Albert Hall

Kensington Palace 6

Map 4B. Kensington Palace Gdns W8. Open daily except 24–26 Dec. Adm charge.

Half of this spacious palace is used as lavish royal apartments; the other half, which includes the 18th-century state rooms, is open to the public. It was converted into a royal palace for William III and his wife Mary by Sir Christopher Wren.

Hyde Park 7

Map 4C. W2. Open daily.

A royal park since 1536, Hyde Park has been a venue for horse racing, duelling, demonstrations, parades and music. The 1851 Exhibition was held here in a vast glass palace. The Princess Diana Memorial fountain is to the south of the Serpentine, while the famous Speakers' Corner is near Marble Arch.

Marble Arch 8

Map 4C. Park Lane W1.

John Nash designed the arch in 1827 as the main entrance to Buckingham Palace, but it was too narrow for the grandest coaches and was moved here in 1851. The arch stands near the site of the old Tyburn gallows, where until 1783 notorious criminals were hanged in public.

Riding on Rotten Row, Hyde Park

STREET LIFE

RESTAURANTS

Isola
Map 5C. 145 Knightsbridge SW1. Tel 020 7838 1044.
Expensive
Italian food in modern setting.

Fifth Floor at Harvey Nichols
Map 5C. 109–125 Knightsbridge SW1. Tel 020 7235 5250.
Moderate
Modern yet intimate restaurant with imaginative menu.

PUBS

Paxton's Head
Map 5C. 153 Knightsbridge SW1.
Old pub catering for all tastes.

SHOPPING

Harrods
Map 5C. 87–135 Brompton Rd SW1.
Upmarket department store.

Burberry
Map 5C. 2 Brompton Rd SW1.
Famous luggage, trenchcoats and other clothing.

Harvey Nichols
Map 5C. 109–125 Knightsbridge SW1.
Designer labels and stylish homeware.

See p96 for price codes.

KENSINGTON AND HOLLAND PARK

The shops in parts of Kensington are almost as smart as those in Knightsbridge. Around Holland Park are some magnificent late Victorian houses, two of them open to the public. But as you cross into Bayswater and Notting Hill you enter a more vibrant, cosmopolitan part of London.

SIGHTS AT A GLANCE

Historic Streets and Buildings
Holland House ❶
Leighton House ❷
Kensington Square ❹
Queensway ❺

Parks and Gardens
Kensington Roof
    Gardens ❸

Markets
Portobello Road ❻

Historic Areas
Notting Hill ❼

SEE ALSO

• *Street Life p83*

KEY

🔵 Underground station

🚉 Railway station

| 0 metres | 500 |
| 0 yards | 500 |

◀ *Entrance to a house in Edwardes Square, Kensington*

Original tiling in Holland House

Holland House ❶

Map 5A. Holland Park W8.

In the 19th century, this was a centre of social and political intrigue. The remains of the house are now a youth hostel. Exhibitions are held in the orangery and the ice house (a forerunner of the fridge), and the old Garden Ballroom is a restaurant.

Leighton House ❷

Map 5A. Holland Park Rd W14. Open Wed–Mon except 25–26 Dec, 1 Jan. Adm charge.

Built for Victorian painter Lord Leighton in 1864–79, the house has been preserved with its opulent decoration as an extraordinary monument to Victorian aesthetics. The Arab hall, added in 1879, houses Leighton's collection of Islamic tiles.

Kensington Roof Gardens ❸

Map 5A. Kensington High Street W8 (entrance in Derry Street). Open daily. Free.

A hundred feet above the bustle of Kensington High Street is a 6,000 sq m (64,580 sq ft) roof garden planted in the 1930s by the owners of Derry and Toms department store below. The display includes a pond

with pink flamingos. It's free to wander round, except when the gardens are booked for events.

Kensington Square ❹

Map 5A. W8.

This is one of London's oldest squares. It was laid out in the 1680s, and a few early 18th-century houses remain. Philosopher John Stuart Mill lived at No. 18, and the Pre-Raphaelite painter Edward Burne-Jones at No. 41.

Resident's plaque in Kensington Square

Queensway ❺

Map 4B. W2.

One of London's most cosmopolitan streets, with a huge selection of eating places. Newsagents are abundantly stocked with foreign newspapers. At the northern end is Whiteley's shopping centre, probably the world's first department

Queensway shop front

store. The street is named after Queen Victoria, who rode here as a princess.

Portobello Road ⑥

Map 4A. W11. Antique market open Fri–Sat.

There has been a market here since 1837. These days the southern end consists almost exclusively of stalls

Antique shop on Portobello Road

that sell antiques, jewellery, souvenirs and many other collectables. The market tends to be very crowded on summer weekends, but it is well worth visiting just to experience its bustling, cheerful atmosphere even if you don't intend buying.

Notting Hill ⑦

Map 4A. W11.

Now the home of Europe's biggest street carnival, most of this area was farmland until the 19th century. In the 1950s and 1960s Notting Hill became a centre for the Caribbean community, many of whom lived here when they first arrived in Britain. The carnival started in 1966 and takes over the area every August during the holiday weekend when costumed parades flood through the streets.

STREET LIFE

RESTAURANTS

Kensington Place
Map 4A. 201 Kensington Church St W8.
Tel 020 7727 3184.
Moderate
A trendy eaterie.

Assaggi
Map 4A. 39 Chepstow Pl W2.
Tel 020 7792 0323.
Expensive
Excellent Italian restaurant.

Clarke's
Map 5A. 124 Kensington High St W8. Tel 020 7221 9225.
Expensive
British and Italian cuisine.

See p96 for price codes.

PUBS AND CAFÉS

Churchill Arms
Map 4A. 119 Kensington Church St W8.
Friendly pub serving Thai food.

The Orangery Tea Rooms
Map 4A. 95–97 Kensington Palace W8.
Serves coffee, teas and lunch.

SHOPPING

The Lacquer Chest
Map 5A. 75 Kensington Church St W8.
Victoriana and Oriental ware.

Barker's
Map 5A. 63 Kensington High St W8.
Various fashion outlets.

REGENT'S PARK AND MARYLEBONE

The area south of Regent's Park has London's highest concentration of quality Georgian housing. Terraces by John Nash adorn the southern edge of Regent's Park, the busiest of the Royal Parks, while to its northwest lies St John's Wood, a smart inner suburb.

SIGHTS AT A GLANCE

Historic Streets and Buildings
Harley Street **3**
Broadcasting House **4**

Museums and Galleries
Wallace Collection **6**
Sherlock Holmes
    Museum **7**

Churches
All Souls, Langham Place **5**

Parks and Gardens
Regent's Park **2**

Attractions
Madame Tussauds and the
    London Planetarium **1**
London Zoo **8**

SEE ALSO

• *Street Life p87*

0 metres   500
0 yards   500

KEY

⊖ Underground station

▣ Railway station

◀ *St Andrew's Place, Regent's Park*

Madame Tussauds and the London Planetarium ❶

Map 2D. Marylebone Rd NW1. Open daily except 25 Dec. Adm charge.

Madame Tussauds still uses traditional wax-modelling techniques to recreate politicians, actors, rock stars and sporting heroes. The Chamber of Horrors depicts episodes of crime and punishment. Next door is the London Planetarium, where a spectacular star show unravels mysteries of the solar system.

Waxwork of Elizabeth II

Regent's Park ❷

Map 2D. NW1. Open daily.

This land became a park in 1812, and John Nash designed the layout. The boating lake teems with water birds and is very romantic, especially when music drifts across from the bandstand. Queen Mary's Gardens are a wonderful sight in summer.

Eminent medical specialists have been here for over a century

Harley Street ❸

Map 3D. W1.

The large houses on this late 18th-century street were popular with successful doctors and specialists in the middle of the 19th century when it was a rich residential area. The doctors' practices lend the street an air of hushed order.

Broadcasting House ❹

Map 3E. Portland Place W1. Not open to the public.

Broadcasting House was built in 1931 as a modern Art Deco headquarters for the then brand-new medium of broadcasting. Its front is dominated by Eric Gill's stylized relief of Prospero and Ariel.

Tulip time at Queen Mary's Gardens in Regent's Park

All Souls, Langham Place ❺

Map 3E. Langham Place W1. Open Mon–Fri, Sun. Free.

Designed in 1824, this is the only John Nash church in London. It had close links with the BBC, and was used as a recording studio for the daily broadcast church service.

Wallace Collection ❻

Map 3D. Manchester Sq W1. Open daily except public hols. Free.

One of finest private collections of European art up to the late 19th century. Among the works is Frans Hals's *The Laughing Cavalier*. There are superb portraits by Reynolds, Gainsborough and Romney. Other highlights are Sèvres porcelain, Houdon and Roubiliac sculptures and a fine collection of European and Oriental armour.

All Souls, Langham Place

Sherlock Holmes Museum ❼

Map 3D. 221b Baker St NW1. Open daily except 25 Dec. Adm charge.

Sir Arthur Conan Doyle's fictional detective lived at 221b Baker Street. This building, from 1815, has been converted to resemble Holmes's flat, and is furnished just as described in the books.

London Zoo ❽

Map 1D. Regent's Park NW1. Open daily except 25 Dec. Adm charge.

A popular attraction, the zoo is also a research and conservation centre. London Zoo has over 600 species of animal, from Sumatran tigers and sloth bears to Mexican red-kneed bird-eating spiders. The astonishing Web of Life exhibit takes you through the vast range of life forms found on Earth.

STREET LIFE

RESTAURANTS

Café Bagatelle
Map 3D. Hertford House, Manchester Sq W1.
Tel 020 7563 9505.
Moderate
Delicious Lunches.

Original Tajines
Map 3D. 7A Dorset St W1.
Tel 020 7935 1545.
Moderate
Hearty tajines and couscous, including vegetarian versions.

See p96 for price codes.

PUBS

O'Conor Don
Map 3D. 88 Marylebone Lane W1. Tel 020 7499 8408.
Genuine Irish pub serving European food with Irish overtones, Guinness and whiskies.

SHOPPING

Divertimenti
Map 3D. 45–47 Wigmore St W1.
Innovative kitchen store.

London Beatles Store
Map 3D. 230 Baker St NW1.
All kinds of Beatles souvenirs.

Further Afield

Surrounding the bustling centre of the capital are some of London's most magnificent and important areas. Graced by famous buildings, parks, museums and other landmarks, good transport links make them easy to reach.

Old Royal Naval College, Greenwich

Greenwich

Train: Greenwich, Maze Hill
DLR: Cutty Sark, Greenwich DLR
LT bus: 188 from Euston
Also numerous riverboats

Greenwich's museums, markets, antique shops, Wren architecture and famous historical sights make for an enjoyable day's excursion.

The National Maritime Museum celebrates Britain's seafaring heritage. A star exhibit is the uniform Lord Nelson was wearing when he was killed at the Battle of Trafalgar. The naval theme continues at the **Old Royal Naval College**, built by Wren. The Hall has opulent ceiling paintings. Greenwich is also home to Greenwich Mean Time, and the meridian passes through the **Royal Observatory Greenwich**. The Observatory houses an intriguing display of astronomical instruments, chronometers and clocks. Finally, **Greenwich Park** has great views from the hilltop.

The National Maritime Museum
Romney Rd SE10. Open daily except 24–26 Dec. Adm charge for special exhibitions.

Old Royal Naval College
Greenwich SE10. Open daily. Free.

Royal Observatory Greenwich
Greenwich Park SE10. Open daily. Adm charge for planetarium shows.

Greenwich Park
SE10. Open daily. Free.

Hampstead

Train: Hampstead Heath
Underground: Hampstead

Essentially a Georgian village, the heath separating Hampstead from Highgate

Hampstead Heath, a welcome retreat from the city

reinforces its appeal, isolating it from the modern city.

Hampstead Heath provides a welcome retreat from the city. Its broad open spaces include ponds and meadows, and on its edges are some historic buildings, including **Kenwood House**. This magnificent Adam mansion is filled with paintings by old masters, such as Vermeer, Turner, Van Dyck and Reynolds.

Hampstead Heath
NW3.

Kenwood House
Hampstead Lane NW3. Open daily except 24–26 Dec, 1 Jan. Free.

Richmond

Train: Richmond (then bus 65)
Underground: Richmond

This attractive London village boasts many early 18th-century houses – notably Maids of Honour

Deer in Richmond Park

Row (1724). Richmond Hill affords beautiful, almost unspoiled views of the river.

Nearby **Richmond Park**, home to herds of red and fallow deer, is the largest royal park at 2,500 acres (1,000 ha).

Richmond Park
Richmond, Surrey. Free.

Kew Palace in Kew Gardens

Kew

Train: Kew Bridge, Kew Gardens
Underground: Kew Gardens

Historic Kew includes the charming riverside walk of Strand on the Green, with its 18th-century houses and famous pubs.

Kew Gardens, also known as the Royal Botanic Gardens, has over 40,000 different species of plants on show.

Kew Gardens
Royal Botanic Gardens, Kew Green, Richmond. Open daily except 25 Dec, 1 Jan. Adm charge.

Hampton Court

Train: Hampton Court

Cardinal Wolsey began building Hampton Court in 1514. Initially intended as Wolsey's riverside home, it was later offered to the king who modified it extensively. The finest piece of Tudor architecture in Britain, its many rooms include a Renaissance picture gallery, the Chapel Royal and fine apartments. Set in 60 acres (24 ha), the gardens, with their famous maze, are an attraction in their own right.

Hampton Court
Surrey. Open daily except 24–26 Dec. Adm charge.

Getting Around

London's public transport system is one of the busiest in Europe, and it has all the overcrowding problems to match. The worst and busiest times to travel are in the two rush hours, between 8am and 9.30am and from 4.30pm to 6.30pm.

The Underground

Known as the Tube, the Underground is usually the fastest way of travelling around, but it can be subject to frustrating delays. The various routes, or lines, are colour coded and easy to follow on the map (see the map on the back of the foldout sheet). Trains run daily, except Christmas Day, from about 5.30am until just after midnight. Fares are based on the six travel zones into which the network is divided.

Underground sign outside a station

Buses

Slower than the Tube but a cheaper way to travel, buses are also a good way of seeing the city. To travel between midnight and 6am, you will need a night bus. All night buses are prefixed with the letter "N" before blue or yellow numbers. All night bus services pass through Trafalgar Square, so head there to get a ride.

Docklands Light Railway (The DLR)

The DLR is an automated overland system serving Docklands. It is linked to the Underground. Outside of rush hour it is a pleasant way to see the East End.

Rail Travel

Suburban and intercity travel is served through the 10 main London termini. Rail travel is expensive and fare structures complicated: for travel in Greater London, Oyster cards and Travelcards offer the most flexibility, while for longer journeys, Cheap Day Returns offer value for money. Cheap Day Returns and Travelcards are only usable after 9.30am. Plan ahead for long journeys.

Buying a Ticket

The most economic tickets are Oyster cards and Travelcards – passes that allow unlimited travel on all forms of transport in the zones you require. You can

The Routemaster bus, which still runs on two 'Heritage' routes

credit Oyster cards with money before your journey. (Six travel zones extend from the city centre; most of London's main sights are in Zone One.) Oyster cards and Travelcards can be bought in Underground or train stations and at newsagents with a red "pass agent" sign. One-day Travelcards cannot be used before 9.30am Monday to Friday. There are no restrictions on weekends.

Driving

Car rental is not cheap and rates are similar among the larger companies. Drivers must show a valid licence and be aged over 21. Driving in London can be slow and parking is hard to find. There is also a daily congestion charge to pay. You must drive on the left.

London on Foot

Walking can be a great option in London. The city centre is compact and distances can be shorter than expected. Be careful when crossing the road. London has two types of pedestrian crossing: striped zebra crossings marked by beacons, and push-button crossings at traffic lights. Traffic should stop

for you if you are at a zebra crossing, but at push-button crossings wait until the green figure lights up.

The traditional London black cab

Taxis and Minicabs

London's black cabs can be hailed anywhere. Their "For Hire" sign lights up when they are free. You can also find them at ranks, near large train stations, airports and some major hotels. A 10 per cent tip is customary. Black cabs can be pre-booked from Radio Taxis and Dial-a-Cab. An alternative to black cabs are minicabs: saloon cars summoned by ringing a firm or going into one of their offices, which are usually open 24 hours. Do not take a mini-cab in the street as they often operate illegally, without proper insurance, and can be dangerous.

TRAVEL INFORMATION

For information about fares, routes and timings of the various transport services, ring 020 7222 1234, check TfL's website **www.tfl.gov.uk** or visit one of the Travel information Centres at Euston, King's Cross and Victoria mainline stations.

The two types of pedestrian crossing instructions

Survival Guide

In this section there is advice about how to stay safe in London, as well as information about money, banks, making phone calls, contacting the police or other emergency services and getting medical or dental assistance if required.

MONEY

Currency

The pound sterling (£) is divided into 100 pence (p). Paper notes are available in denominations of £5, £10, £20 and £50. Coins are 1p, 2p, 5p, 10p, 20p, 50p, £1 and £2.

Banks

Banks are generally open 9.30am–4.30pm Monday to Friday. Most banks and building societies have cash machines (ATMs) for use outside opening hours.

A cashpoint machine

Bureau de Change

Bureau de Change are regulated, and their rates are displayed along with commission charges.

Credit Cards

Most UK establishments accept major credit cards. Credit cards can also be used to obtain cash, using a PIN number.

COMMUNICATIONS

Postal Services

Post offices are generally open from 9am–5.30pm Monday to Friday and until 12.30pm on Saturday. You can also buy stamps in shops, hotels and other outlets. • Royal Mail Customer Help Line: 0845 774 0740. www.royal mail.co.uk

Telephones

Most phone boxes take coins (30p minimum) and credit cards. If you have difficulty contacting a number, call the Operator (100) or International Operator (155). In an emergency, dial 999 or 112. The code for London is 020, which you omit when dialling within the city. To call abroad from London, dial 00 followed by the access code of the country you are dialling. • Directory Enquiries: 118 500 • International Directory Enquiries: 118 505

Faxes and Photocopiers

There are fax and photo-copying shops throughout London, and many hotels also offer these facilities.

Internet

There are a number of Internet bars and cafés throughout London.

Post boxes with collection times

HEALTH

Hospitals
There are several hospitals in central London with 24-hour emergency services, including dental hospitals.

Pharmacies
Pharmacies (chemists) are open during business hours, some until late, and can advise on minor ailments.

Dentists
Hotels can usually suggest local dentists, and many are listed in Yellow Pages. For free emergency treatment go to Guy's Hospital Dental Department.

Sexual Health
St Thomas's, Westminster and St Mary's Hospital, Paddington, have walk-in clinics that deal with sexually transmitted diseases.
• Aids Helpline: 0800 567 123.

SAFETY

Emergency
For emergency police, fire or ambulance services dial

LONDON HOSPITALS

St Mary's
Praed Street W2
• 020 7886 6666
St Thomas's
Lambeth Palace Road SE1
• 020 7188 7188
University College
Gower Street WC1
• 020 7387 9300
Guy's Hospital Dental Department
St Thomas Street SE1
• 020 7118 7188
NHS Direct
24-hour nurse-led advice line
• 0845 4647

Boots pharmacy

999 – the operator will ask which service you require. This number is free on any public telephone.

Theft
You should be especially vigilant late at night and in poorly populated areas or back streets. Look after possessions, keeping valuables concealed. Keep hold of your bag in pubs and other public places. Make sure your possessions are insured before you arrive and, if possible, leave valuables in the hotel safe. Report all thefts to the police, especially if you will need to make an insurance claim.
• West End Central Police: 27 Savile Row W1 (tel 020 7437 1212).

Lost Property
Anything found on the tube or buses is sent to the London Transport Lost Property Office.
• Transport for London Lost Property: 200 Baker Street NW1 (tel 020 7918 2000).

A police constable

Index

Acknowledgments

Dorling Kindersley would like to thank the following people whose help and assistance contributed to the preparation of this book.

Design and Editorial
Publisher Douglas Amrine
Publishing Manager Vivien Antwi
Managing Art Editor Kate Poole
Cartography Casper Morris
Design Kavita Saha, Shahid Mahmood
Editorial Dora Whitaker
Production Controller Shane Higgins
Picture Research Ellen Root
DTP Jane Little
Jacket Design Simon Oon, Tessa Bindloss.

Julie Bowles, Caroline Mead, Pete Quinlan, Mani Ramaswamy, Sadie Smith, Sylvia Tombesi-Walton.

Picture Credits

Every effort has been made to trace the copyright holders, and we apologize in advance for any omissions. We would be pleased to insert appropriate acknowledgments in any subsequent edition of this publication.

t = top; tl = top left; tc = top centre; tr = top right; cla = centre left above; ca = centre above; cra = centre right above; cl = centre left; c = centre; cr = centre right; clb = centre left below; cb = centre below; crb = centre right below; bl = bottom left; b = bottom; bc = bottom centre; br = bottom right.

The Publishers are grateful to the following individuals, companies and picture libraries for permission to reproduce their photographs:

AXIOM: James Morris 58t; GETTY IMAGES: Image Bank/Romilly Lockyer 21c; ROBERT HARDING PICTURE LIBRARY: Mark Mawson 32; JOHN HESELTINE: 40, 46, 84; REDBACK PUBLISHING: 20cla, 20clb, 20br, 21t, 21br; PHILIP WAY PHOTOGRAPHY 65; ZEFA IMAGES: 7c.

JACKET
Front – GETTY IMAGES: Photographer's Choice/ David Sutherland.
Spine – Stone/John Lawrence front.

All other images © DORLING KINDERSLEY
For further information see www.DKimages.com.

Price Codes are for a three-course meal per person including tax, service and half a bottle of house wine (unless required to supply your own).
Cheap under £15
Moderate £15–£35
Expensive £35 or more

SPECIAL EDITIONS OF DK TRAVEL GUIDES

DK Travel Guides can be purchased in bulk quantities at discounted prices for use in promotions or as premiums. We are also able to offer special editions and personalized jackets, corporate imprints, and excerpts from all of our books, tailored specifically to meet your own needs.

To find out more, please contact:
(in the United States)
SpecialSales@dk.com
(in the UK) **Sarah.Burgess@dk.com**
(in Canada) DK Special Sales at
general@tourmaline.ca
(in Australia) **business.development@pearson.com.au**